Grammar Mastery —for Better Writing

Workbook Level 2

Curriculum Unit
Mary Louise Wanamaker

The Center for Learning

The Center for Learning
www.centerforlearning.org

The Author

Mary Louise Wanamaker, who earned her M.A. at St. Louis University, has taught English, grades 9–12, to all ability levels. She concentrated on developing curriculum during her sixteen years as principal. Wanamaker also has twelve years' experience as a teacher supervisor at Province High Schools, Los Angeles, where she worked with principals on curriculum matters.

The Editorial Team

Diana Culbertson, Ph.D.
Amy Hollis, B.S.J.
Rose Schaffer, M.A.
Bernadette Vetter, M.A.

Cover Design

Susan Sheaffer Curtis, B.A.

Copyright ©1997 The Center for Learning, Cleveland, Ohio.
Second edition 2000. Reprinted 2012.

Manufactured in the United States of America.

ISBN-13: 978-1-56077-630-7
ISBN-10: 1-56077-630-7

Contents

To the Student

This is a workbook that you will use over and over. It contains valuable information that will help you develop your writing skills, pass achievement tests, and make your college English class a snap.

The purpose of this unit is to give you techniques that will help you to write naturally and correctly. The focus is on all aspects of complex structures: clauses, sentences, transitions, parallel forms, indirect and direct discourse, sentence variety, correct usage, elimination of deadwood, and punctuation. You will learn sentence expanding and combining. Many exercises are provided for drill and reinforcement. Each new concept stems from what has been taught, thus providing a constant review.

At the completion of this course, you should be able to concentrate on the content of your writing rather than grammatical correctness. Your sentences should be more mature, and your own style of writing should gradually develop. A growing confidence in your ability to express yourself clearly and succinctly will be a source of untold benefits for your future studies and for your chosen career. So be of good heart, tackle the material, and come out a winner!

Unit 1
Basic Materials

Basic Patterns

First Basic Pattern

The first basic pattern consists of subject and intransitive verb. The subject is always the doer, and the action is complete in itself.

> The men *worked* in the field around the clock.
>
> My friend *played* in the band for three years.

Second Basic Pattern

The second basic pattern consists of subject and transitive verb. The subject can be the doer or the receiver. When the subject is the doer, the verb is speaking actively. When the subject is the receiver, the verb is speaking passively.

Subject as the doer, active voice:

> John *found* his ball in the yard.

Subject as the receiver, passive voice:

> The ball *was found* in the yard.

Third Basic Pattern

The third basic pattern consists of subject, linking verb, and subject complement. The subject complement is sometimes called the predicate nominative (if it is a noun or pronoun) or a predicate adjective. The subject is neither the doer nor the receiver. The verb is neither active nor passive.

> Tom will be editor-in-chief for another year.

Tom and *editor-in-chief* are linked by the linking verb *will be*.

> My mother is a good *cook*. (noun)
>
> Bob was very *despondent* over the accident. (adjective)

Exercise 1

Directions: Write *I* for intransitive, *T* for transitive, or *L* for linking.

Example: <u>*L*</u>   The best player was he.

_____1.   I met my grandmother for dinner last week.

_____2.   She was the best runner in our class.

_____3.   He had a comfortable room.

_____4.   The book report was finished on time.

_____5.   Jeannie sings beautifully.

_____6.   The cat's eyes were green in the dark.

_____7.   The climbers proceeded cautiously up the mountain.

_____8.   Farmers must have water during the drought.

_____9.   My sister jumped quickly into the car.

_____10. Tom became the school's mascot.

_____11. Clara studied hard for the test.

_____12. My sick brother feels miserable.

_____13. My camera takes great pictures.

_____14. We rested by the fire all evening.

_____15. My hands feel sticky.

_____16. Al was gentle with his dog.

_____17. My parakeet talks incessantly.

_____18. The gym was beautifully decorated.

_____19. We all went to the dance.

_____20. John met the mayor at the reception.

Exercise 2

Directions: Write out the basic patterns of the following sentences.

Example: Those green apples taste bitter. *Apples taste bitter.*

1. The wind blew off our roof.

2. Jim, the captain of the basketball team, will represent the team at the meeting.

3. The coach took his football team to the USC game.

4. Jim should have been our first choice for captain.

5. We visited Mr. Stafford, president of our Booster Club.

6. The salesman sold me a fantastic stereo.

7. My mother's pie crusts are always light and flaky.

8. The students entered the auditorium and sat down quietly.

9. We received very little information about the accident.

10. We greeted the President in Washington, D.C.

Subject-Verb Agreement

The subject always controls the verb. A singular subject takes a singular verb; a plural subject takes a plural verb. A prepositional phrase seldom controls the subject.

> The *boy* with his sisters *is leaving*.

When using correlatives, the noun that follows *or* or *nor* controls the verb.

> Bob or his *friends are planning* to hold a surprise party for the coach.

> His friends or *Bob is planning* to hold a surprise party for the coach.

A linking verb must agree with its subject, regardless of the number of its predicate nominative.

> Speeding *cars are* one reason for the accident.

> One *reason* for the accident *is* speeding cars.

The indefinite pronouns *each, every, neither, either, one,* or *body* are always singular.

The indefinite pronouns *both, few, many, others,* and *several* are always plural.

Some, most, none, all, and fractions are either singular or plural depending on the prepositional phrase that follows.

> All of the *apples were eaten* yesterday.

> All of the *apple was eaten* by the horse.

Exercise 3

Directions: Write the letter of the correct answer.

Example: <u>B</u>   Most of the pies (A. was B. were) sold during the first hour of the fair.

_____1.   Jerry and Tom (A. is B. are) going to win the contest.

_____2.   The girls on our committee (A. have B. has) arrived early.

_____3.   Bacon and eggs (A. is B. are) my favorite breakfast.

_____4.   Tom with his sisters (A. have B. has) gone to Europe.

_____5.   Many a man, woman, and child (A. have B. has) been fooled by con artists.

_____6.   The girls or the boys (A. expect B. expects) to win the race.

_____7.   There (A. is B. are) several reasons for his leaving early.

_____8.   On the bottom shelf (A. is B. are) several old sweaters.

_____9.   Economics (A. was B. were) Bob's major.

_____10. The jury (A. have B. has) left their seats.

_____11. The problem at our school's outing (A. was B. were) the bees.

_____12. Politics (A. have B. has) always interested me.

_____13. All the teachers (A. have B. has) voiced their reasons for his acceptance.

_____14. *Green Mansions* (A. is B. are) his favorite novel.

_____15. Only one reason for his absence (A. was B. were) given.

_____16. Everyone in our class (A. has B. have) promised to attend the play.

_____17. In the back of the room (A. is B. are) several empty boxes.

_____18. A box of typewriting ribbons (A. was B. were) sent to the missions.

_____19. Both the twins and Mary (A. is B. are) receiving flu shots today.

_____20. My favorite meal (A. are B. is) spaghetti.

_____21 The news (A. has B. have) not been good for weeks.

_____22. Three-fifths of the money (A. was B. were) given to charity.

_____23. One-tenth of the accidents (A. have B. has) been caused by drunk drivers.

_____24. A number of planes (A. was B. were) lost in battle.

_____25. The number of students interested in physics (A. has B. have) increased each year.

_____26. One of our television sets (A. is B. are) broken.

_____27. A trip to Europe or Asia (A. is B. are) dangerous at this time.

_____28. There (A. have B. has) been several attempts on his life.

_____29. Ten dollars (A. is B. are) too much to spend for that book.

_____30. Each of these papers (A. is B. are) well written.

_____31. All of the candy (A. has B. have) been sold.

_____32. Sixty-five pennies (A. is B. are) lying on the desk.

_____33. The number of applications (A. exceed B. exceeds) the number of positions available.

_____34. Sixty cents (A. is B. are) the cost of that notebook.

_____35. None of my valuables (A. was B. were) stolen.

Case: Nouns and Pronouns

All nouns have case. Because pronouns take the place of nouns, they also have case. Nouns do not change form when they change case.

> John (nominative case) saw Peter (direct object) in the theater (object of a preposition).

Nouns in the possessive case add _'s_ to nouns that do not end in _s_ and _'_ to plural nouns that end in _s_. Singular nouns that end in _s_ ordinarily add _'s_.

> John's room   The girls' toys   James's hat

Exceptions include Jesus (_Jesus' words_) and Moses (_Moses' law_).

Unlike nouns, personal pronouns have different forms to show whether they are in the nominative case, the objective case, or the possessive case.

Nominative Case	**Singular**	**Plural**
First person	I	we
Second person	you	you
Third person	he, she, it	they

Objective Case		
First person	me	us
Second person	you	you
Third person	him, her, it	them

Possessive Case		
First person	my, mine	our, ours
Second person	your	yours
Third person	his, her, its	theirs

Exercise 4

Directions: Write the letter of the correct pronoun on the first line at the left. On the second line, write *N* for nominative case, *O* for objective case, or *P* for possessive case.

Example: _B_ _O_ Everyone saw (A. he B. him) at the concert.

____ _____ 1. (A. They B. Them) left early for the show.

____ _____ 2. It was (A. she B. her) entering the building.

____ _____ 3. Before entering the room, (A. we B. us) waved to them.

____ _____ 4. Let's you and (A. I B. me) go to the rally.

____ _____ 5. The teacher gave (A. he B. him) a letter of recommendation.

____ _____ 6. The book belongs to (A. he B. him).

____ _____ 7. It was (A. his' B. his) idea in the first place.

____ _____ 8. To (A. she B. her) belongs the credit.

____ _____ 9. It must have been (A. they B. them) at the rally.

____ _____ 10. Bess gave (A. she B. her) all the answers.

____ _____ 11. Divide the money between Tom and (A. he B. him).

____ _____ 12. It was (A. theirs' B. theirs) to begin with.

____ _____ 13. The (A. children's B. childrens') work was displayed.

____ _____ 14. (A. It's B. Its) nest was built on a rock.

____ _____ 15. It could have been (A. I B. me) at the mall.

____ _____ 16. Please send (A. she B. her) the assignment.

____ _____ 17. The book is (A. your's B. yours).

____ _____ 18. The door fell off (A. it's B. its) hinges.

____ _____ 19. The principal told (A. we B. us) his plans.

____ _____ 20. Aunt Louise told mother and (A. I B. me) the news.

____ _____ 21. The best speaker was (A. he B. him).

____ _____ 22. The director liked (A. my B. me) singing.

____ _____ 23. Between (A. we B. us) there is no peace.

____ _____ 24. Is (A. she B. her) going to Hawaii?

____ _____ 25. (A. Ladies' B. Ladie's) dresses were on sale.

Exercise 5

Part A.

Directions: Complete the sentences with a pronoun in the correct case.

Example: _I_ She and _____ went shopping after school.

_____ 1. John and ____ plan to visit Boston this summer.

_____ 2. Let's go visit _____ grandmother.

_____ 3. My boss promoted my brother and _____ .

_____ 4. The best students in ___ class are Tom and Shelly.

_____ 5. _____ voted for Beth and Jim.

_____ 6. She gave Tom's sister and _____ the report.

_____ 7. Did you see Al and _____ playing tennis?

_____ 8. Between _____ there are no secrets.

_____ 9. We need _____ help.

_____ 10. _____ thought the show was over.

Part B.

Directions: Complete the sentences with either *who* or *whom*.

Example: *Who* won the contest?

11. _____ will be leaving early?

12. Of _____ were you speaking?

13. _____ is the president of your class?

14. _____ did you expect to see at the party?

15. To _____ was she referring?

16. _____ will they choose?

17. _____ rang the fire bell?

18. _____ will you choose to represent the class?

19. _____ is the best French teacher?

20. The best speaker was_____ ?

Exercise 6

Pronoun and Antecedent Agreement

Part A.

Directions: Write the letter of the correct pronoun.

Example: *A* One of my sisters took (A. her B. their) dog for a walk.

_____1. One of my friends left (A. his B. their) jacket at my house.

_____2. Some of the actors forgot (A. his B. their) lines.

_____3. All of my friends finished (A. his B. their) assignment.

_____4. Several of the players gave (A. his B. their) autographs.

_____5. Neither of the girls gave me (A. her B. their) notes.

_____6. Only one of the teachers explained (A. her B. their) marking system.

_____7. Not one of the players gave us (A. his B. their) reasons for not responding to the questionnaire.

_____8. Both Tom and Mary left (A. her B. their) books in the gym after basketball practice.

_____9. Which one of the students brought (A. his B. their) car for the field trip?

_____10. Either Mary or Jennifer will read (A. her B. their) story to the class on Monday.

Compound Personal Pronouns

Intensive pronouns are used for emphasis. They can be omitted without changing the meaning of the sentence.

> I *myself* want to give the speech.
>
> He did it *himself*.

Reflexive pronouns are used as complements (direct object). They are always a part of the sentence.

> Julio hurt *himself*.
>
> My brother shaved *himself* for the first time this morning.

Never use a compound personal pronoun without its antecedent.

Part B.

Directions: Correct the misused reflexive pronouns in the following sentences. If there is no error, mark it correct.

Example: Herself did it yesterday. *She did it yesterday.*

11. The teacher wants Bob and myself to enter the speech contest next month.

12. The best tennis player is yourself.

13. He injured himself in the game last night.

14. Neither Bob nor myself want to go to the tournament.

15. Either John or myself will host the party.

16. I did it myself.

17. She gave Paul and myself the good news.

18. I myself will take care of cleaning up after the party.

19. You should learn to take the pictures yourself.

20. Jason and myself will present the problem to the faculty members for a solution.

Verbals

A *verbal* is a word derived from a verb. Like a verb, it can be modified and have one or more compliments. However, it does not function as a verb.

A verbal with modifiers and/or complements is a *verbal phrase.* Verbals used like noun are called *gerunds.* Verbals used like adjectives are called *participles.* Verbals that modify nouns, adjectives, and adverbs are called *infinitives.* The sign of the infinitive is *to.*

Gerunds

A gerund is a verbal noun. It has one form: *verb + ing.*

        walking   giving

A gerund with its modifiers is a gerund phrase. Because it is a noun, it has case.

Subject

        Writing poetry is his favorite hobby.

        Working with my father can be frustrating.

Direct Object

        My little sister enjoys swimming.

        We started working in the library last month.

Subject Complement (also called Predicate Nominative)

        His hobby is sorting stamps.

        John's fear was joining the army.

Appositions

        Her job, correcting papers, can be tedious.

        Her hobby, collecting stamps, is also educational.

Indirect Object

        His lecture gave speaking a new dimension.

        His writings made traveling an exciting experience.

Object of a Preposition

        He had no intention of writing his autobiography.

        We learned of his leaving for Africa.

Participles

A participle is a verbal adjective. As an adjective, it must modify a noun. It has tense and voice.

	Active	**Passive**
Present	giving	being given
Past	——	given
Perfect	having given	having been given

        Giving his lunch money to his friend, Bob left the cafeteria.

Giving modifies *Bob.*

        My car, having been fixed, now runs smoothly.

Having been fixed modifies *car.*

        Having washed his car, Tom took his friend to McDonald's.

Having washed modifies *Tom.*

Dangling Participles

A participle dangles when it modifies the wrong noun.

> Locked in his kennel, I was annoyed by my dog's barking.

> Badly needing sleep, my eyes could hardly stay open.

Infinitives

An infinitive is a verbal usually preceded by *to*, the sign of the infinitive.

> to write   to play

Infinitives can be used like nouns, adjectives, or adverbs.

Noun

Subject	To exercise daily is good for everyone.
Direct Object	Bill wanted to survive the war.
Subject Complement (Predicate Nominative)	His desire was to survive the war.
Object of Preposition	He had no alternative except to forgive.
Apposition	His hobby, to travel, costs money.

Adjective	The person to notify is your nearest relative.
Adverb	We will be happy to serve you.

Omitting the Sign of the Infinitive

Sometimes the sign of the infinitive can be omitted.

> The policeman made the spectators move. (to move)

> Please help me bake a cake. (to bake)

The noun or pronoun in front of the infinitive is always in the objective case.

> He made them to move.

> The principal asked them to leave.

When the infinitive is linking, the complement refers to the assumed subject of the infinitive, which is in the objective case.

> We knew the best *actress* to be *her*.

> The principal believed the best *student* to be *him*.

Punctuating Verbals

Participles

1. When a participle or a participial phrase starts the sentence, always follow it with a comma.

    > Working to finish the project on time, John stayed up all night.

2. When the participle restricts the noun, do not use a comma.

    > The boy playing in the street was hit by a car.

    The participial phrase is necessary to the meaning of the sentence because it answers the question *which one*.

3. When the participial phrase is not necessary to restrict the noun (that is, to answer the question *which one*), use commas to set it off.

    > Peter, playing in the street, was hit by a car.

There are no special rules for gerunds and infinitives.

Exercise 7

Part A.

Directions: Write *G* for gerund, *P* for participle, or *I* for infinitive.

Example: *P*   The teacher sponsoring an art project received many commendations.

_____1.   *Searching* for the truth, Bob did hours of research.

_____2.   He decided *to attend* the convention in Atlantic City.

_____3.   The professor had no intention of *leaving* early.

_____4.   *Winning* the competition is the dream of every coach.

_____5.   I enjoy *skiing* at Big Bear.

_____6.   *To succeed* in business you must often take a chance.

_____7.   The principal does not plan *to enter* the contest.

_____8.   The sheriff made the men *move* immediately.

_____9.   The club asked her *to give* the opening talk.

_____10. We will let them *share* our lunch.

_____11. *Waiting* in line for tickets to the concert can be frustrating.

_____12. *Waiting* in line for two hours, we finally left.

_____13. *Delighted* with his singing, they hired him on the spot.

_____14. Everyone wants the music *to stop*.

_____15. Do you enjoy *studying* English?

_____16. He bought the pictures *to decorate* his home.

_____17. You can also buy other materials for *decorating* your house.

_____18. After *working* for that company for ten years, I was fired.

_____19. Do you expect me *to believe* your story?

_____20. *Playing* tennis is really enjoyable.

_____21. *Having broken* his arm, Bud went to the hospital.

_____22. *Preparing* for the journey, we took five suitcases.

_____23. We saw him *walking* toward the bridge.

_____24. His *speaking* brought tears to my eyes.

_____25. Judy wanted her brother *to send* her a letter.

_____26. Everyone wants credit for *trying*.

_____27. *Planning* for your future is a necessity.

_____28. *Frightened* by the noise, I ran into the house.

_____29. We chopped the celery in small pieces *to add* texture.

_____30. She doesn't dare *leave* home without her parents' permission.

_____31. I need Jill *to help* me with the report.

_____32. *Dancing* can help you lose weight.

_____33. His house, *shaded* by oak trees, is generally cool.

_____34. His performance gives *acting* a bad name.

_____35. We enjoy *camping* during the summer.

Part B.

Directions: Write *P* if the underlined word is part of the progressive verb, or *G* for a gerund.

Example: _P_   She is going to the store.

    ____36. Their hobby is *climbing* mountains.

    ____37. She has been *enjoying* her job for over a month.

    ____38. Her favorite pastime is *watching* TV.

    ____39. Don's greatest accomplishment was *winning* the short story contest.

    ____40. He was *writing* his short story for two months.

    ____41. Henry is *going* to Paris.

    ____42. My best subject is *writing*.

    ____43. His mistake was *joking* with Mr. Pendergast.

    ____44. He is *playing* tennis this afternoon

    ____45. My chief concern was *stopping* the flow of blood.

Phrases

A **phrase** is a group of words that functions as a single grammatical unit. It is always dependent. In our study of the simple sentence, we also studied many types of phrases.

Types of Phrases

1. *Prepositional phrase*

   On the child's face glowed an expression *of exquisite joy.*

2. *Verb phrase*

   Paul *has* already *left* for Europe.

3. *Participial phrase*

   The old man crouched in a dark corner *rubbing his hands for warmth.*

4. *Infinitive phrase*

   To accomplish much in a short time requires concentration.

5. *Gerund phrase*

   The old lady delights in *checking all the garbage cans in her neighborhood.*

6. *Appositive*

   Mr. Peabody, *my old chemistry teacher,* visited our school last week.

7. *Adverb noun*

   Kay visited her mother *last week.*

Exercise 8

Directions: Name the type of the italicized phrase.

Example: _Infinitive phrase_   I met her *to discuss our plans.*

    _____ 1. *After writing the report,* I returned the books to the library.

    _____ 2. John, *my friend,* plans to go to USCB in the fall.

    _____ 3. None of her money *had been stolen.*

    _____ 4. My friends and I left immediately *after the game.*

_____5. *Joining the Marines* takes courage and dedication.

_____6. *To eat correctly* is important for one's health.

_____7. Ted enjoyed *working on his computer*.

_____8. She *should have written* that letter sooner.

_____9. She wanted *him to leave the dance immediately*.

_____10. He made *us clean the entire yard*.

_____11. Tom, *the best player on the team*, injured his back yesterday during the game.

_____12. Mary ran *into the house* singing joyfully.

_____13. They were not allowed *to write on the blackboard*.

_____14. At the air show yesterday, we met David Burns, *a former prisoner of war in Saudi Arabia*.

_____15. We all enjoyed *visiting the Santa Barbara Mission*.

_____16. *Before studying at UCLA*, I attended Kent State University.

_____17. After we helped *them build the dog house*, we celebrated at Pizza Hut.

_____18. Jim, *my first cousin*, will graduate from Stafford University.

_____19. My father helped *me climb the ladder to our attic*.

_____20. *Playing tennis in the heat* gave me a headache.

_____21. Joe saw the accident *from the freeway*.

_____22. My mother came into the room with a plate *filled with delicious chocolate cookies*.

_____23. We decided to build a house *with three large bedrooms*.

_____24. Jessie Jones, *my friend since first grade*, is now a high school teacher.

_____25. Ellen was proud of *working for my uncle*.

Phrases and Modifiers Expand Basic Patterns

Tom laughed.

Tom, my guest from Arizona, laughed heartily at the joke.

(Added an appositive, an adverb, and a prepositional phrase.)

Bob broke arm.

During football practice, Bob, tackling Albert, the quarterback, broke his arm in two places.

(Added two prepositional phrases, a participial phrase, and two appositives.)

Ruth is champion.

My sister Ruth, an avid tennis player, is now amateur champion of Minnesota.

(Added five adjectives, an appositive, and a prepositional phrase.)

Directions: On a separate sheet of paper, expand the basic patterns and indicate what kind of phrase or modifiers you used. Do not change the basic pattern.

Example: Card made dad happy.

The card for Father's Day, beautifully designed by my sister, made my dad very happy.

(Added two prepositional phrases, a participial phrase, and two adverbs)

1. Child ran.
2. We arrived.
3. Nickname is Bubba.
4. Jerry gave suggestions.
5. Teacher wrote letter.
6. Living was difficult.
7. Susan wore necklace.
8. Air felt wonderful.
9. We showed cousin the zoo.
10. Everyone enjoyed picnic.
11. Friend and I visited Museum.
12. Dick found book.
13. John volunteers.
14. Football team won.
15. Family went to Florida.

Objective Complement

An objective complement is a word that completes the direct object. A complement can be a noun, an adjective, or (infrequently) a pronoun. An objective complement is used with such verbs as *appoint, name, think, call, make, consider, elect,* and *render.* (It often includes the idea "to be," as in *We elected Mary* [to be] *president.*)

The teacher considered the boy a genius.

Subject: *teacher*

Transitive verb: *considered*

Direct object: *boy*

Noun complements the direct object: *genius*

The news made Jim unhappy.

Subject: *News*

Transitive verb: *made*

Direct object: *Jim*

Adjective, complements the direct object: *unhappy*

They called the park his.

Subject: *They*

Transitive verb: *called*

Direct object: *park*

Pronoun, complements the direct object: *his*

Distinguishing between Modifiers and Complements

Modifier

A modifier is never a part of the basic pattern. A modifier always modifies a noun or a verb. It is generally an adjective or an adverb. A modifier is never necessary to the meaning of the sentence.

Jean wore a red dress.

Red is a modifier, describing *dress*.

Mother baked a delicious pie.

Delicious is a modifier describing *pie*.

Complement

A complement completes the transitive verb, the preposition, the direct object, or the subject (when the verb is linking). It is generally a noun or an adjective, sometimes a pronoun.

She walked quickly down the street.

Street, a noun, is a complement of the preposition *down*; it completes the preposition.

Ed painted the fence white.

White, an adjective, is a complement of the direct object *fence*; it tells what color he painted the fence.

Exercise 10

Directions: Write *M* for modifier or *C* for complement for the italicized words.

Example: _C_ Alvin broke his *pencil*.

_____1. Her father became very *strict* after the accident.

_____2. Jane made her room *comfortable*.

_____3. Tom painted his *white* room light green.

_____4. She was *happy* with her new job.

_____5. The coach made Tom very *happy*.

_____6. I read an *exciting* novel.

_____7. My *millionaire* brother is going to Europe.

_____8. Nero made Rome *beautiful*.

_____9. The teacher called Ted *wise*.

_____10. Mr. Smith is a *wise* teacher.

_____11. I called that car a *beauty*.

_____12. She wore a *bright blue* dress.

_____13. The rainbow was *beautiful*.

_____14. She drives a *silver* car.

_____15. I lost an *expensive* bracelet.

_____16. He called the bracelet *expensive*.

_____17. The downpour was *terrible*.

_____18. His story sounded *preposterous*.

_____19. Mabel called her husband *stubborn*.

_____20. I bought a *gorgeous* prom dress.

Directions: Write out the basic patterns of the following sentences.

Example: Mary, my cousin, painted her room a pale yellow. *Mary (cousin) painted room yellow.*

1. The company made Clarence their new chief.

2. Bob and Carol made their house comfortable.

3. She painted the garage a bright purple.

4. Jean called her brother a nuisance.

5. Please consider the proposition open for discussion.

6. The principal made Gina chairperson of the English department.

7. The beautician made Terry's hair curly.

8. The school chose Jody as its homecoming queen.

9. My mother named my little brother Ted.

10. The president appointed his friend social director.

Position of the Objective Complement

The objective complement usually follows the direct object.

> The blow stretched him senseless on the floor.

Subject: *blow*

Transitive verb: *stretched*

Direct object: *him*

Objective complement: *senseless*

Sometimes the objective complement follows the transitive verb, and the direct object is placed last. This pattern is often used for emphasis.

> The rain will sweep clean all the streets.

Subject: *rain*

Transitive verb: *will sweep*

Direct object: *streets*

Objective complement: *clean*

Sometimes the objective complement is placed first in the sentence and the direct object is last.

> A perpetual fountain of good sense Dryden called Chaucer.

Subject: *Dryden*

Transitive verb: *called*

Direct object: *Chaucer*

Objective complement: *fountain*

Exercise 12

Directions: For the italicized words, write *S* for subject complement, *O* for objective complement, or *D* for direct object.

Example: <u>*S*</u>   Jerry's house is *green*.

_____1.   The teacher chose Jose the best *writer* in the class.

_____2.   Louise laid bare her *plans* to her friends.

_____3.   Wordsworth made the commonplace *marvelous*.

_____4.   Did they elect *Janice* captain of the softball team?

_____5.   That coat was too *small* for her.

_____6.   He remained a *hermit* for twenty years.

_____7.   He appointed his *brother* his guardian.

_____8.   Dancing practice has never made him *graceful*.

_____9.   My father and Mr. Jones are business *partners*.

_____10. He called his pain a *headache*.

_____11. Did you see *Paul* at the show?

_____12. Paul is a very astute young *man*.

_____13. Everyone labeled Ed a *winner*.

_____14. The media called him a *villain*.

_____15. Iago is a *villain* in every sense of the word.

_____16. Jerry met the *villain* in a dark alley.

_____17. They were world-famous *architects*.

_____18. The company named Terry the *architect* of the year.

_____19. Sharon was an *architect* of great renown.

_____20. John met *Sharon* at the Architect's Convention.

_____21. Did you see *Pete* on the golf course?

_____22. Pete is an outstanding *golfer*.

_____23. Golf requires a *lot* of strategy.

_____24. We named Pete the *golfer* of the school.

_____25. *Fantastic* is what they called him.

Nominative Absolute

The term *absolute* means "not dependent on anything," "standing apart," or "standing alone."

Sometimes the noun or pronoun modified by a participle or a participial phrase stands apart from the rest of the sentence. It is not a part of the subject or the predicate; in other words, it is not grammatically connected to the sentence, but it is closely related in thought. It indicates the time, reason, or circumstance for the rest of the sentence. It also lends variety in writing. This phrase is called a **nominative absolute**.

> The rain was falling. Tom took his umbrella. (Two sentences)
>
> Taking his umbrella, Tom went out into the rain. (Participial phrase modifying the subject, *Tom*)
>
> Rain falling, Tom took his umbrella. (*Rain falling* is an absolute; it is not connected grammatically to the sentence. *Rain* is in the nominative case.

An absolute always stands alone. An absolute never modifies any part of the sentence.

> Her purse stolen, Patricia, sobbing with grief, ran home.

The phrase *her purse stolen* stands alone. It is a nominative absolute.

Sometimes the participle *being* is omitted from the nominative absolute, but it is always understood.

> Hand in the cookie jar, my little brother was caught in the act.
>
> *Hand being in the cookie jar*, my little brother was caught in the act.
>
> Jane slept all day, her temperature over 100 degrees.
>
> Jane slept all day, *her temperature being over 100 degrees.*

A nominative absolute compresses writing.

> We stumbled along. The snow crunched under our feet.
>
> *Snow crunching under our feet, we stumbled along.*
>
> The dog was lying at his feet. Roger whittled a stick.
>
> *The dog lying at his feet, Roger whittled a stick.*

Because a nominative absolute is never a part of the sentence, it is always separated with commas.

> Tom, his eyes smarting from the smoke, left the building.
>
> His eyes smarting from the smoke, Tom left the building.
>
> Tom left the building, his eyes smarting from the smoke.

Exercise 13

Directions: If the sentence contains an absolute, write *A*. If not, write *B*.

Example: *A* The wind blowing, we struggled to reach home.

_____1. The day being cold, John brought a sweater.

_____2. Helmet fixed firmly on his head, Ted took a ride on his motorcycle.

_____3. Entering the room cautiously, Paul investigated the unusual noise.

_____4. Telling jokes at the meeting, Jon made his boss unhappy.

_____5. The expensive vase broken, Mary and Joe hid the pieces.

_____6. The lifeguard, using his megaphone, yelled at us.

_____7. The lifeguard yelling, we swam to shore.

_____8. The telephone wires destroyed by the storm, we had no electricity for ten hours.

_____9. Stuck in traffic, everyone kept honking his horn.

_____10. The traffic halted, everyone kept honking his horn.

_____11. Thinking quickly, she applied the brakes.

_____12. The storm growing in intensity, we went to the cellar.

_____13. Running to catch the bus, John tripped and fell.

_____14. Shaded by many trees, our house is generally cool.

_____15. Our house shaded by many trees, we enjoyed comfortable temperatures.

_____16. Worried, Joan called her mother immediately.

_____17. Our dog Brandy, bounding up the steps, almost knocked me over.

_____18. The sun setting over the ocean, we took pictures of the beautiful sunset.

_____19. John, his feet pounding rhythmically, carried the ball for thirty yards.

_____20. Frightened by the change in the weather, I ran into the house and hid under my bed.

_____21. Splashing water on the spectators, the dolphins seemed to enjoy their screams.

_____22. The dolphins splashing water, the spectators screamed and ran in great excitement.

_____23. Mary, her skates broken, was forced to resign from the contest that she had hoped to win.

_____24. Whirling on one skate, Michelle gave a great performance to the delight of the spectators.

_____25. The tires on our old Ford, worn almost threadbare, had to be replaced.

Exercise 14

Directions: On a separate sheet of paper, write five good sentences using nominative absolutes.

Exercise 15

Directions: On a separate sheet of paper, write three good sentences using participles.

Unit 2 Adverb Clauses

Clauses

A **clause** is a group of words with a subject and a predicate. There are two kinds of clauses: Independent (main or principal) and Dependent (subordinate).

Independent Clause

The independent clause is a simple sentence. It has a subject and a predicate and expresses a complete thought. The simple sentence was reviewed in the opening section of this workbook.

Exercise 16

Directions: Write *C* for an independent clause or *P* for a phrase.

Example: <u>C</u>   I spent an hour in the museum.

_____1. The beautiful painting on display at the Huntington Museum and worth over two million dollars.

_____2. Jumping about excitedly at the good news broadcasted last night.

_____3. Stop immediately!

_____4. Urging his team to victory, the coach gave a powerful pep talk in the locker room.

_____5. The person to see about a job at the Edison Company's main plant.

_____6. Neither Mabel nor the twins enjoy watching soccer.

_____7. Shopping at the mall every Saturday morning can be tiresome.

_____8. A beautiful balmy day in early February with light breezes and much sunshine bringing a feeling of well being to everyone.

_____9. The wind showed no signs of abating.

_____10. Carefully surveying the shoreline, he spotted a whale in the distance.

Exercise 17

Directions: On a separate sheet of paper, write simple sentences using the following words.

1.	believing	11.	striking
2.	us to see	12.	telling
3.	digging	13.	completed
4.	running	14.	giving
5.	broken	15.	lay
6.	write	16.	having found
7.	me to give	17.	has arrived
8.	during	18.	wrapping
9.	had been left	19.	have seen
10.	lying	20.	sailing

Exercise 18

Directions: Indicate how the italicized word or words are used in these sentences.

Example: _preposition_   I started my homework *after* dinner.

_____ 1. Bob tore his shirt *wrestling* in the gym.

_____ 2. The *wrapping* paper was a dark green.

_____ 3. *Sailing* in his canoe, Tim fell overboard.

_____ 4. He hid in the cellar *during* the storm.

_____ 5. I wanted her *to leave* immediately.

_____ 6. *Reading* the textbook carefully will help in a test.

_____ 7. Jim *had taken* the book to the library.

_____ 8. Jon enjoys *sailing*.

Dependent Clause

The dependent (subordinate) clause has a subject and a predicate, but it does not express a complete thought. It depends on the main (principal) clause for its full meaning.

> If you lost that money

This clause has a subject and a predicate, but its meaning is not complete. It needs a principal clause to complete its meaning.

> *If you lost that money,* we can't go to the movies.

Exercise 19

Directions: If the clause is complete, write *C*; if it is incomplete, write *I*.

Example: _C_   Before I could finish speaking, she interrupted me.

_____1. While I was reclining in that easy chair.

_____2. Order me an ice cream soda.

_____3. Please bring your book to class tomorrow.

_____4. So that we could attend the rally.

_____5. If the mud slides continue.

_____6. Although I had studied practically all night.

_____7. Please get your brakes fixed.

_____8. Slowly he raised the glass to his lips.

_____9. I saw the entire accident clearly.

_____10. Laughing continually until he lost his breath.

_____11. Wherever she was and whatever she did.

_____12. Since she does not have a driver's license.

_____13. While you were studying in your room last night.

_____14. Before you turn in your next assignment in English.

_____15. When you finish the assignment.

_____16. As long as you sit there pouting and fretting.

_____17. Jean studied the plans of the building very carefully.

_____18. Laughing at the joke, Brian gasped for breath.

_____19. Laughing is good for the health.

_____20. Before the day was over.

Adverb Clauses

An **adverb clause** is a dependent clause. Like adverbs, it modifies a verb, an adjective, or another adverb answering such questions as *why, when, where, how, to what extent, in what manner, and under what conditions.* However, you can generally recognize an adverb clause because it is introduced by a subordinate conjunction.

A **subordinate conjunction** always reduces an independent clause to a dependent clause.

> We won the football game last night.

This is a complete sentence. If a subordinate conjunction is added to this sentence, it would no longer be independent.

> After we won the football game last night.

This clause no longer expresses a complete thought; it depends on another clause to complete it. *After* is a subordinate conjunction reducing the independent clause to a dependent clause.

> Because we won the football game last night.

This is a dependent adverb clause. *Because* is a subordinate conjunction making the clause dependent.

The most common subordinate conjunctions:

after	though	where	even though
although	unless	wherever	in order that
as	until	while	so that
because	when	that	provided that
since	whenever	as long as	as if

Exercise 20

Directions: Reduce the following independent clauses to adverb clauses by adding subordinate conjunctions.

Example: She wants to study engineering. *Because she wants to study engineering*

1. He ate his breakfast this morning in the cafeteria.

2. She will go to Arizona State in the fall.

3.   Fred did not see the car coming toward him.

4.   Jane finds walking very difficult.

5.   She studies very hard.

6.   Our team will go to Magic Mountain in May.

7.   Ted enjoys working at Fox Studio.

8.   He did research for his science project.

9.   She is taking German at night school.

10. She made many errors in spelling.

Exercise 21

Directions: Add adverb clauses to the following principal clauses. Put parentheses around your subordinate conjunction.

Example: We won the game. *We won the game (even though) the referee favored the other team.*

1.   My older sister will lose her job.

2.   Tom became very ill.

3.   We decided to go to the school concert early.

4.   Our house was painted white.

5. I telephoned you yesterday.

6. Al refused to answer the door.

7. Maryann kept on working.

8. My aunt decided to stay with us for another month.

9. Larry will go to college.

10. Copy this material in your notebook.

Exercise 22

Directions: Write the subordinate conjunction.

Example: *after*   I understood the concept after reviewing the chapter.

_____ 1. Unless you study, you will certainly fail.

_____ 2. He can go provided he has done his homework.

_____ 3. Men go where angels fear to tread.

_____ 4. My brother is always good when he is sleeping.

_____ 5. You better finish that report by tonight if you don't want to be disqualified.

_____ 6. Running when you are exhausted is foolish.

_____ 7. She left early because she was extremely tired.

_____ 8. Send me the final report when you are finished.

_____ 9. My mother gave me ten dollars because I did well on my final exam in math.

_____ 10. We practiced all evening so that we could win the prize.

_____ 11. Since he entered this school, he is a different person.

_____ 12. Join the club if you want to have a good time.

_____ 13. I feel much better than I did yesterday.

_____ 14. Even though my best friend was ill, I enjoyed the party.

_____ 15. I will go with you whenever you want.

Periodic or Loose Sentences

When an adverb clause comes first in the sentence, the sentence is classified as periodic (the main clause ends with a period). When the sentence is periodic, always use a comma.

When you leave the room, please lock the door.

If you want to pass the final exam, you will have to study.

When the adverb clause ends the sentence, the sentence is classified as loose (the main clause comes first). Do not use commas except for clarity.

Take the books to the library *before they are overdue.*

Joe was determined to play *even though he was sick.*

For writing purposes, it doesn't matter whether your sentences are periodic or loose. Periodic sentences are excellent for emphasis and for keeping the punch line at the end.

Exercise 23

Directions: Write *P* for periodic or *L* for loose. Punctuate correctly, and underline the subordinate conjunction.

Example: *P*   <u>Although</u> Jean was upset over the incident, she did not show it.

_____1. My mother telephoned me before she left for Canada.

_____2. If you call before ten o'clock leave a message.

_____3. She remained in the room until I had finished the essay.

_____4. Although Bob is a good writer he often makes careless mistakes.

_____5. Check over your examination paper before you hand it in.

_____6. Unless you make a different choice I will not sponsor you.

_____7. Because she is stubborn and because she will not listen to others she often causes untold difficulties.

_____8. You can go provided you are home by 1:00 A.M.

_____9. Although it was still early we decided to leave.

_____10. You will have no friends as long as you have that negative attitude.

_____11. If you make the team you must be willing to practice every day.

_____12. Did you meet Tom my cousin when you were in San Diego?

_____13. I will go with you as soon as I get my sweater.

_____14. Because Jan won the nomination we were all delighted.

_____15. We left early in order to get good seats.

Exercise 24

Directions: Combine the following sentences by changing independent clauses to dependent adverb clauses. Try to vary periodic and loose sentences.

Example: We could not go on the picnic. My little sister had the chicken pox. *We could not go on the picnic because my little sister had the chicken pox.*

1. I was waiting for Bob to call. I jumped every time the phone rang.

2. We were sailing on the lake. Suddenly a rainstorm came.

3. My little sister wandered into the street. She was almost hit by my brother's car.

4. The telephone rang. My sister ran to the phone.

5. We set the alarm clock. We did not want to oversleep.

6. She will lose her job. She is too slow and careless.

7. I went to see Manuel last week. He is seriously ill in the hospital.

8. Jane cried practically all evening. Her parakeet died.

9. You should be able to get a good job. You know word processing.

10. We stood around and talked. We barbecued hamburgers and hot dogs.

11. Show Jake the door. He is making a nuisance of himself.

12. Bob received a demerit. He has been disturbing the class all period.

13. We notified the paramedics immediately. We saw the accident.

14. Put the book on the shelf. That is where you found it.

15. Jerry had collected all the data. He wrote an excellent term paper.

Verb Sequence with Adverb Clauses

When the main verbs in the main clause and in the adverb clause are in the past tense, but the time of the action is not simultaneous, the earlier verb must be in the past perfect tense.

Before we witnessed the accident, John was driving erratically.

In this sentence, *witnessed* occurs before *was driving*. The earliest action must be in the past perfect tense.

Before we witnessed the accident, John *had been driving* erratically.

Mr. Jones bought a new house after he returned from the East.

Mr. Jones bought a new house after he *had returned* from the East.

Exercise 25

Directions: Mark the verbs *A* for the earliest action or *B* for the later action. Then rewrite the sentence correctly.

Example: Before I *saw* <u>B</u> the movie, I *read* <u>A</u> the book.

Before I saw the movie, I had read the book.

1. Pete *studied* _____ for days before he *took* _____ his exam.

2. After he *gathered* __ ___ the material, he *wrote* _____ his essay.

3. Before she *graduated* ___ from UCLA, Margaret *worked* _____ for my father.

4. I *returned* _____ to the classroom before he *called* ___ for me.

5. After he *stole* _____ the money, he *left* _____ the country.

6. Arthur *sneezed* _____ and *coughed* _____ a lot before he *moved* _____ to Arizona.

7. Unless he *wrote* _____ the letter, he *could not be prosecuted* _____ .

8. My brother *went* _____ to boot camp after he *joined* _____ the army.

9. Although our team *made* ____ five home runs, the Pirates *won* ____ the game.

10. Before he *accepted* ____ his new job, Jim *asked* ____ for all its requirements.

Elliptical Adverb Clauses

An **elliptical adverb clause** is a clause in which the subject or the verb or both are understood but not actually stated. Elliptical writing or speaking is economy of speech.

Even though the subject or the subject and verb are omitted, they still function to make the clause express a complete thought.

> Tom runs faster than I. (*run* is understood)
> Tom throws the ball farther than Ted. (*throws the ball* is understood)
> Mary likes him better than me. (*she likes* is understood)

Exercise 26

Directions: Complete the adverb clause by adding the missing words.

Example: Joe is a better writer than I. *than I am a writer*

1. Tim enjoys football more than I.

2. Alice works as hard as Mary.

3. Barbara likes me better than her.

4. Our basketball team is better than theirs.

5. Bob runs faster than Jim.

6. My father likes baseball more than soccer.

7. Jean is not as kind as her twin.

8. Our math class needed more assistance than his.

9. Arthur enjoys typing more than algebra.

10. John is more pessimistic than I.

11. Jill works harder than she.

12. California is larger than Arizona.

13. I enjoy her concerts more than his.

14. Paul is a better pianist than Jeannie.

15. Jake is as tall as my brother.

16. He is wiser than Ted.

17. John needs more help than she.

18. The teacher likes Joe better than me.

19. Bob is better at tennis than she.

20. Jack studies harder than she.

Than and *as* are subordinate conjunctions that are frequently used in elliptical clauses.

> She is better than I.
>
> Joe is as good in math as she.

While and *when* are subordinate conjunctions also used in elliptical clauses.

> While studying for my exam, I got a severe headache.
>
> *While I was studying for my exam,* I got a severe headache.
>
> Be sure to visit Fisherman's Wharf when in San Francisco.
>
> Be sure to visit Fisherman's Wharf *when you are in San Francisco.*

Exercise 27

Directions: Write out the complete adverb clause.

Example: When sailing on the bay, Brian enjoys the breeze and warm sunshine.
When he is sailing on the bay,

1. When filling in your applications, be sure to sign your names.

2. While fixing his car, John hurt his arm.

3. When planting marigolds, keep them away from open windows.

4. Ted is a better writer than Greg.

5. Peggy enjoys swimming more than Carl.

6. He requires more help than Jerry.

7. While snorkeling, she saw two large crabs.

8. My mother is two years older than my father.

9. Jerry understands math better than Jim.

10. While swimming in the lake, Ruth got a severe cramp in her leg.

11. When called, you should answer immediately.

12. Mr. Smith is a better math teacher than Mr. Jones.

13. Bob hits the ball farther than Ted.

14. When eating lunch in the cafeteria, be sure to put your dishes away.

15. Martha is happier in her married life than Jill.

16. While studying for the exam, Peter plays his radio at full blast.

17. When applying for a job, be sure to dress professionally.

18. When handing in your papers, always check over your material.

19. She enjoys taking care of children more than I.

20. When playing ball in the park, do not leave food wrappers around.

21. Bob is taller than he.

22. He enjoys music lessons more than I.

23. Millie is more mature than Jack.

24. While eating lunch, Bob swallowed a bone.

25. Never eat when playing the piano.

Subordination

Subordination is the joining of two ideas or facts, one of which is more important or needs more emphasis than the other. The most important fact should be expressed in the independent clause; the less important fact should be expressed in the dependent clause.

It is a priority in writing to understand the importance of subordination. Facts that are joined are not always of equal importance and should not be given equal emphasis.

> I went to the city, and I bought a coat and dress.

In this sentence the writer is using compound sentences, making the ideas of equal importance.

> *I went to the city. I bought a coat and dress.*

The sentence would be better if the first clause were subordinated.

> When I went to the city, I bought a coat and dress.

> We are a people in a democracy, and we control things, and therefore, our beliefs are important.

In this sentence all the ideas are of equal importance, and seemingly just strung together.

> In a democracy where we, the people, control things, our beliefs are important.

Note the subordination: *where we, the people, control things*. The writer then emphasizes the main idea: *our beliefs are important.*

> The book was well written even though the plot was poor.

The emphasis in this sentence is *the book was well written.*

> The plot was poor even though the book was well written.

The emphasis in this sentence is *the plot was poor.*

The emphasis of your paragraph or topic will help you determine which sentences need to be put in subordinate positions.

Exercise 28

Directions: Join the following sentences together by using subordinate conjunctions. Your sentences may be periodic or loose. Be sure to punctuate correctly.

Example: I liked the movie. I guessed the ending right away. *I liked the movie even though I guessed the ending right away.*

1. Paul wrote a long letter to his mother. He wanted to explain the reasons for not writing to her before.

2. Lincoln High School is rather small. It has one of the best football teams in the state.

3. The last sound of hoofs died away. Everything now seemed calm and safe.

4. The stage crew worked long hours building the scenery for *The Wizard of Oz*. They wanted everything to be perfect.

5. *The Glass Menagerie* by Tennessee Williams has a powerful opening scene. Tom, both a character in the play and the narrator, steps into the limelight and addresses the audience.

6. Everyone enjoyed the softball game very much. It was full of excitement and thrills with a tied score up to the last inning.

7. The boys entered the cave cautiously. It was dark and damp with an atmosphere of mystery.

8. The examination room was filled with apprehensive students. Tense and excited, they milled around waiting for directions.

9. Doctors always made John nervous and unhappy. He squirmed, fidgeted, and cried every time he had to go.

10. Our club has won many trophies and medals. We still need more members.

Review

Independent and Dependent Clauses

An independent clause has a subject and predicate and makes a complete statement.

A dependent clause has a subject and predicate, but it is dependent on an independent clause to complete its meaning.

Adverb Clauses

An adverb clause is a dependent clause which modifies a verb, an adjective, or another adverb. An adverb clause is always introduced by a subordinate conjunction. A subordinate conjunction reduces an independent clause to a dependent clause.

An adverb clause can be periodic or loose. It is periodic when the subordinate conjunction introduces the sentence. In periodic sentences, use commas after the adverb clause.

The adverb clause is loose when it ends the sentence. No comma is necessary.

An elliptical adverb clause is a clause in which the subject or the verb or both are understood but not actually stated. Even though the subject or the subject and verb are omitted, they still function to make the clause express a complete thought.

Subordination joins two ideas or facts, one of which is more important or needs more emphasis than the other. Always make the most important fact the independent clause, and the less important the adverb clause.

Exercise 29

Part A.

Directions: Underline the subordinate conjunction.

Example: <u>When</u> Larry erases the board, he always has to show off.

1. We were determined to win the tournament so that we could get a computer.

2. Tim studied French every night since he wanted to visit Paris next summer.

3. The entire sophomore class was happy when Bill won the election.

4. John is taller than Fred.

5. Playing basketball, if you have talent, can give you many fringe benefits.

6. We plan to go to Canada this summer because my father's sister lives there.

7. Jean wrote her essay very carefully so that the teacher would enter it into the English contest.

8. Although there were many people auditioning for the play, John easily received a part.

9. Working hard until his project was finished, Bob received an A.

10. Working for my uncle last summer, I earned enough money to buy a car.

Part B.

Directions: Write *P* if the sentence is periodic or *L* if it is loose.

Example: *L*　My mother was worried when my sister did not call her.

_____11. If you studied as hard as you play, you would be an honor student.

_____12. Bob could not get the job because he had only a high school diploma.

_____13. Unless the job is finished by midnight, we will lose money.

_____14. While playing soccer, Jack sprained his ankle.

_____15. Since you are not interested in the concert, we will give Tom your ticket.

_____16. Mary is a better tennis player than Jane.

_____17. You will get the promotion if you pass the written exam.

_____18. You can't join the glee club unless you audition.

_____19. Before you sign up for his class, you must take a test.

_____20. Although Tom is a good tennis player, he is not dedicated enough to become the best.

Part C.

Directions: Finish the following sentences by adding adverb clauses. Underline your subordinate conjunction.

Example: We are going to the game, <u>*since*</u> *the concert was cancelled.*

21. Our basketball team is better

22. My mother telephoned the doctor in the middle of the night

23. My niece is going to Arizona University

24. Everyone in the bus wanted to go to Yosemite

25. Bill hurt his elbow yesterday

26. Jill is more famous

27. Always look out

28. The teacher did nothing about his disrespectful manner

29. I hope to finish this essay tonight

30. He ran

Unit 3
Adjective Clauses

Relative Pronouns

Adjective clauses are dependent clauses. Like adjectives, they modify nouns or pronouns. Because they are always related to a noun or pronoun, they are also classified as relative clauses.

An adjective clause is introduced by a relative pronoun either stated or understood. The relative pronouns are *who, whom, which, that,* and *whose.*

The relative pronouns *who* and *whom* always refer to a person.

> boy who

> Mary about whom

The relative pronouns *that* and *which* refer to things. Although often used interchangeably, *which* is correctly used in nonrestrictive clauses. *That* specifically identifies the antecedent and is used in restrictive clauses.

> house which

> book that

Whose is a relative adjective modifying a noun and relating to a person.

> The lady *whose purse was stolen* went to the police.

A relative clause always gives more details about the noun it modifies.

> Mary applied for the secretarial job yesterday.

> Mary, *who majored in business,* applied for the secretarial job yesterday.

> The dog had no collar or license.

> The dog *that was picked up by the dog catcher* had no collar or license.

Functions of Relative Pronouns

1. Relative pronouns connect relative clauses to the word or words they modify.

2. Relative pronouns agree with the words they modify in number and gender.

3. The relative pronoun does not necessarily agree in case with the word it modifies.

> The book (nominative) that (objective) I lost has been found.

4. The relative pronoun should follow the noun it modifies as closely as possible.

> We visited Tom's house last week that he bought two months ago.

The relative clause *that he bought two months ago* modifies *house.* It would be better to rewrite the sentence so that the relative clause follows *house.*

> Last week we visited Tom's house that he bought two months ago.

5. Relative pronouns have case.

Subject

The window *that was broken* was expensive.

That is the subject of the verb *was damaged*.

Direct Object

The actress *whom you saw yesterday* is an active environmentalist.

Whom is the direct object of the verb *saw*.

Object of Preposition

The story *about which you spoke* will be made into a movie.

Which is the object of the preposition *about*.

Relative Adjective

The man *whose job was in jeopardy* appealed to the company's president.

Whose is a relative adjective modifying *job* but relating to *man*.

Exercise 30

Directions: Underline the relative clause in each sentence and write on the line the word that the clause modifies.

Example: *girl*   The girl <u>to whom</u> I <u>wrote</u> moved to Korea.

_____ 1. A box of oranges that was shipped last week has never arrived.

_____ 2. My sister-in-law, who lives in Florida, will be visiting us next week.

_____ 3. We knew the policeman who gave us a ticket.

_____ 4. The house that Jack build was destroyed by fire.

_____ 5. Our basketball team, which is still undefeated, will play for the championship next Friday.

_____ 6. My aunt, whose term of office will end in January, plans to live in Paris.

_____ 7. The dog that my father gave me for my birthday is now just six months old.

_____ 8. *A Tale of Two Cities*, which we studied last year, gives a detailed picture of the French Revolution.

_____ 9. He sat on the chair that my brother had just painted.

_____ 10. My ring that I lost several weeks ago was returned last night.

Adjective Clauses

A relative pronoun or adjective introduces an adjective clause. A relative pronoun is always a part of a relative clause: subject, direct object, or object of a preposition. It is related to the noun it modifies.

Adverb Clauses

Subordinate conjunctions introduce adverb clauses. They reduce an independent clause to a dependent clause. The subordinate conjunction is not a part of the adverb clause.

Exercise 31

Directions: Write *ADV* for adverb clause or *ADJ* for adjective clause.

Example: <u>*ADJ*</u>   The coat that she bought yesterday has a small defect.

_____1. *Although Ted was a good student,* he could not get a job.

_____2. *Since you will be leaving in the fall,* may I have your books?

_____3. The article *that you sent me last week* is most valuable for my research paper.

_____4. My cousin, *who is an excellent seamstress,* will make my wedding dress.

_____5. *If you plan to publish your poetry,* please call my uncle.

_____6. Leave early *if you are bored.*

_____7. Professor Smith, *to whom you gave your story,* sent it to a professor who teaches at Harvard.

_____8. The money *that my father sent me last week* was lost in the mail.

_____9. All the material *that we bought last year* is now depleted.

_____10. The policeman found the girl *who was kidnapped.*

Exercise 32

Directions: Write out the relative pronoun and indicate its use: *S*, subject; *DO*, direct object; *OP*, object of a preposition; or *R*, relative adjective. Then write out the antecedent.

Example: <u>*whom*</u> <u>*OP*</u> <u>*boy*</u> The boy to whom I spoke is both an athlete and an honor student.

_____ _____ _____ 1. I read the letter that came from my cousin.

_____ _____ _____ 2. The girl to whom I gave the letter never mailed it.

_____ _____ _____ 3. The movie which lasted two hours was boring.

_____ _____ _____ 4. The position that my sister wanted was filled some time ago.

_____ _____ _____ 5. Borg, whose tennis playing was masterful, was the top player for several years.

_____ _____ _____ 6. The bicycle that I bought has great speed.

———— —— ———— 7. The photographs that he took last week are not yet developed.

———— —— ———— 8. Did you find the video that we needed for class?

———— —— ———— 9. They can subpoena anyone whom they choose.

———— —— ———— 10. The novel that I like the best was *The Perfect Stranger.*

———— —— ———— 11. My best friend, whose father was transferred to India, will live with me.

———— —— ———— 12. Bob introduced me to the professor about whom he spoke so eloquently.

———— —— ———— 13. The novel that you recommended is not in the library.

———— —— ———— 14. I lost the bracelet that Jake gave me for my birthday.

———— —— ———— 15. Everyone who attended the workshop received extra credit.

———— —— ———— 16. The project that he made for his science class was sent to state competition.

———— —— ———— 17. We found the book that you lost.

———— —— ———— 18. Aunt Jane, whose interest in theater is almost fanatical, goes to every show in town.

———— —— ———— 19. The relatives whom they visited were all from Peru.

———— —— ———— 20. The news that was on TV last night was exciting.

———— —— ———— 21. The report that I gave my teacher received an A.

———— —— ———— 22. This is the bedroom about which I have been speaking.

———— —— ———— 23. Jane, whose book is about to be published, is also an artist.

———— —— ———— 24. Did you read the poem that Jim wrote?

———— —— ———— 25. The scene in which the boy got the girl is the best.

Relative Pronouns Omitted

Sometimes a relative pronoun is omitted. The missing pronoun, however, is understood and still functions in the sentence.

> The flowers I bought for my mother are beautiful.

The relative pronoun *that* is understood even though it is not stated.

A relative pronoun is understood when you can supply it in your mind or the dependent clause needs a word to introduce it.

> The friends I visited are my cousins. (whom I visited)

> The article I needed could not be found. (that I needed)

Exercise 33

Directions: Rewrite the following sentences and supply the understood relative pronoun. Underline the relative clause.

Example: The poster she gave me is hanging on my wall. *The poster* that <u>she gave me</u> *is hanging on my wall.*

1. The bicycle Tim bought is red and blue.

2. The gifts Gerry received at her wedding were fantastic.

3. The jacket my mother bought last week is light blue.

4. The car he damaged has been repaired.

5. The importance he placed on his talk was ridiculous.

6. The car my brother bought is his prized possession.

Relative Adverbs

A **relative adverb** modifies a noun.

The adverb *where* follows a place.

park where	room where
house where	city where

The adverb *when* follows an expression of time.

second when	week when
minute when	year when

The adverb *why* follows a reason.

The reason why she left is not known.

Exercise 34

Directions: Underline the relative clauses in the following sentences.

Example: The store <u>where</u> <u>I</u> <u>used</u> <u>to</u> <u>work</u> closed last year.

1. The book I bought for my mother last year is now out of print.

2. The clothes that were shipped to the missions were damaged in transit.

3. We all visited the zoo where we saw many kinds of animals.

4. The flowers that I took to the hospital were for my cousin Joe.

5. The news that was on the radio spoke of a flood in Germany.

6. Did you meet Tom Selleck, who was on the plane with you?

7. I can see no reason why I should go to New York.

8. It was the exact moment when the accident happened.

9. The paint that I needed so desperately never arrived.

10. The prison where he spent the last twenty years burned down.

11. The dog that I received for my birthday is a golden retriever.

12. The box in which I put the jewelry is misplaced.

13. The talk that he gave to his students really motivated them.

14. The announcement that school would close for a week startled everyone.

15. My third quarter report card that the school sent to my parents had three As.

Nonrestrictive and Restrictive Adjective Clauses

Nonrestrictive Adjective Clauses

Nonrestrictive adjective clauses are not necessary in the sentence to restrict the nouns they modify. When clauses are not necessary to restrict their antecedent, they must be set off with commas. **Restricted nouns** are proper nouns, or nouns already restricted by other modifiers, such as *Albert* or *gold bracelet*.

John, who wants to go to the Naval Academy, needs a 4.0 GPA.

John is a restricted noun, so the phrase *who wants to go to the Naval Academy* is not necessary to restrict it and commas are needed. The meaning of the sentence is clear without the clause.

Mr. Jones, who teaches me algebra, is a terrific teacher.

Mr. Jones is already restricted, so *who teaches me algebra,* is not necessary to restrict it and commas are needed. The meaning of the sentence is clear. The clause does not answer the question *which one.*

Restrictive Adjective Clauses

An adjective clause that is needed to restrict a noun is necessary and should not be set off with commas.

A student who wants to go to the Naval Academy needs a 4.0 GPA.

Student is not restricted, so the phrase is necessary and no commas are used.

The man who teaches me algebra is a terrific teacher.

Man is not restricted, so the phrase is necessary and no commas are used.

Exercise 35

Directions: If the noun is already restricted, write *R*; if it is not restricted, write *N*.

Example: *R*   Uncle Jack

_____1. Jerry		_____11. piano
_____2. dishes		_____12. John Wayne
_____3. Jim		_____13. my brother
_____4. the Alamo		_____14. leader
_____5. doctor		_____15. her bracelet
_____6. this city		_____16. museum
_____7. magazine		_____17. Kelly
_____8. novel		_____18. apple pie
_____9. my brother		_____19. his cousin
_____10. Yosemite		_____20. Shakespeare

Other names for *restrictive* and *nonrestrictive* are *essential* and *nonessential*. When the clause is essential, that is, it restricts its antecedent, do not use commas. When the clause is nonessential, that is, it does not restrict its antecedent, use commas.

Analyzing Restrictive and Nonrestrictive Relative Clauses

The girl who won the tennis match is my sister.

Girl is not restricted. It needs a clause to restrict it. The clause *who won the tennis match* is necessary to restrict *girl*. Because the clause is necessary, do not use commas.

My father, who is a professional tennis player, won five tournaments.

Father is restricted by *my*. The clause *who is a professional tennis player* is not necessary to restrict *father*. It does not answer the question *which one*. Use commas to set off the clause from the rest of the sentence.

Exercise 36

Directions: Analyze the following sentences to determine whether the clause is restrictive or nonrestrictive. Punctuate correctly.

Example: Mary who is an excellent pianist will study piano at college.

Antecedent is Mary, restricted. Clause is nonrestrictive. Use commas.

Mary, who is an excellent pianist, will study piano at college.

1. The boy who broke his leg was a football player.

2. The kitten that I brought home yesterday loves our house.

3. Tom who is my best friend will be moving to Australia.

4. Professor Jones who is an excellent teacher has been my teacher for two years.

5. The ring that I found in the park was claimed by three people.

6. The book that I bought at the store is damaged.

7. My essay which won first prize will be sent to Washington, D.C.

8. The papers that were lost have been found.

9. Jerry's bike which was damaged in the accident has been repaired.

10. The umbrella that was lying in the ditch is now useless.

Directions: If the clause that follows the noun restricts the noun, write *R*. If the clause does not restrict the noun, write *N*. Punctuate correctly.

Example: _R_   The building that is on Fourth Street was sold last week.

_____1. Our basketball coach who was honored at a banquet last night is an outstanding coach.

_____2. My term paper on which I spent many hours received only a B.

_____3. Paul who is a famous soccer player will play in Hawaii next spring.

_____4. The store sells a wide variety of bracelets that are made by the Sioux tribe.

_____5. Any chemist who knows the formula can give you accurate information.

_____6. The man who gave us a tour of the museum was very knowledgeable.

_____7. Albert who always sees good in everything and everyone speaks kindly even about his worst enemy.

_____8. Some roads that the Romans built are still in use.

_____9. The first Superbowl Game which was played in 1967 was held in the Los Angeles Coliseum.

_____10. We found all the materials that you had lost in the files in your office.

_____11. Mary whose essay on citizenship was outstanding hopes to be a journalist someday.

_____12. The composer who wrote this music is truly a genius.

_____13. The hummingbird whose needle-sharp bill can drive off crows and hawks is a fearless fighter.

_____14. I met Cindy who is from Dallas, Texas.

_____15. Galileo who made observations about the sun eventually became blind.

Review

Phrases that modify nouns can be either restrictive or nonrestrictive.

1. *Participles*

   If the participle modifies a restricted noun, use commas.

   If the participle modifies a nonrestricted noun, do not use commas.

2. *Apposition*

   Apposition can also restrict or not restrict its antecedent.

Exercise 38

Directions: If the clause or phrase is restrictive, write *R*. If it is not restrictive, write *N*. Punctuate correctly.

Example: *R*   The girl running across the street is Joe's sister.

_____1. The article written by Jim is worth reading.

_____2. The book *Madame Bovary* is not in our library.

_____3. My brother who practices six hours each day is a champion swimmer.

_____4. The man working as a security guard was injured yesterday.

_____5. The boy riding the bicycle goes to Williams High School.

_____6. The coat given to me for my birthday is very expensive.

_____7. We saw the play *The King and I* last Friday night.

_____8. Bob who works at McDonald's is saving his money for college.

_____9. Jerry leaving his books in his locker ran quickly to the football field.

_____10. My math teacher joining us for the party has a great sense of humor.

Exercise 39

Directions: Combine the following sentences by using relative clauses.

Example: Our class read *Macbeth*. It is a play by Shakespeare.

   Our class read Macbeth, *which is a play by Shakespeare.*

1. My mother and cousin visited President Reagan's library. It is in Simi Valley.

2. John won a trip to Spain. He will be leaving in July.

3. Our dog was seriously injured last night. He was struck by a car.

4. James left for Mexico yesterday. He will be introduced to a special youth team there. (Use a relative adverb.)

5. His beautiful home was destroyed by fire. He built his home just three years ago.

6. Mr. Appleton arrived for a conference. He is the guest speaker for the occasion.

7. Have you met Mr. Gonzales? He will be the new Spanish teacher next semester.

8. My friends and I have always wanted to see *Sunset Boulevard*. It is no longer playing in Los Angeles.

9. Rebecca, my sister, plans to write novels in the future. She is an avid reader.

10. Jack is studying photography. He enjoys taking pictures.

11. I am planning to visit my uncle in Japan this summer. My uncle loves to travel.

12. They held their conference in Chicago. It is a windy city.

13. His house was destroyed by a tornado last week. It will take months to rebuild it.

14. Gary wants to study art and photography in summer school. He plans to major in graphic arts in college.

15. My friend's mother loves to sew. She makes many of our clothes.

Exercise 40

Directions: Write *R* for restrictive or *N* for nonrestrictive. Punctuate correctly.

Example: <u>*R*</u>   The sweater that my aunt gave me is too big.

_____1.   The audience who attended the play was rude and boisterous.

_____2.   The box that was lying on the counter belongs to Ned.

_____3.   The book that we read last year was *A Separate Peace*.

_____4.   Jill who is an excellent pitcher helped us win the championship.

_____5.   His parents who are very strict would not let him attend the play.

_____6.   The dog that ran across the street was hit by a car.

_____7. Jack who is majoring in math plans to go into research.

_____8. The water that I took with me on the hike was lukewarm.

_____9. Jane who is in the first grade is already a good reader.

_____10. The desk that is in my father's room needs a coat of varnish.

_____11. The paper that is lying on the teacher's desk belongs to Bob.

_____12. My computer which was just purchased last year won't work.

_____13. Jerry who is a great baseball player is moving to Canada.

_____14. We read the report that was in the magazine.

_____15. The pamphlets that we collected yesterday were distributed throughout the city.

_____16. We all read the article that was in _The Times_.

_____17. The window that was installed in our store yesterday cost almost a thousand dollars.

_____18. My bedroom which needed painting badly now looks like new.

_____19. Our class visited the art museum which has an exhibit of Impressionist paintings.

_____20. Our golf team which was in last place in the league last year won the city championship this year.

Exercise 41

Directions: Put parentheses around the relative clause and underline the antecedent.

Example: Student <u>projects</u> (that involve research on the Internet) are becoming more commonplace.

1. Computers that have already taken over in the business world are also now a must in classrooms and libraries.

2. Processing centers will disperse information that the home computers request.

3. Many schools have added computer programs that help young people learn.

4. Computers have changed the work habits of people who work in offices.

5. Many people whose jobs are in offices are now starting to work in their homes.

6. Students who use computers seem to understand concepts easier.

7. First graders are now using computers that help them write.

8. My brother has a computer that helps him with his calculus.

9. Many hospitals today have computers that detect diseases.

10. My cousin, who studies medicine, uses a computer daily.

Directions: Write out the relative pronoun and indicate its use: *S*, subject; *DO*, direct object; *OP*, object of a preposition; or *R*, relative adjective. Then write out the antecedent.

Example: *that*   *S*   *roses*   The roses that grow in my garden are American Beauties.

_____ _____ _____   1. A career as a doctor might be considered by students whose interest is medicine.

_____ _____ _____   2. A book on careers that I saw in the library gave me some helpful advice.

_____ _____ _____   3. The man to whom I gave a book about medicine became a broadcaster.

_____ _____ _____   4. Many jobs that require long hours of work are frequently ignored.

_____ _____ _____   5. My father, who is an engineer, is noted for his work.

_____ _____ _____   6. Many companies hire people who have knowledge of computer programs.

_____ _____ _____   7. I visited a studio that specializes in cartoons.

_____ _____ _____   8. My little sister loves to go to Disneyland, which is a playground for millions.

_____ _____ _____   9. The museum that specializes in modern art has many wealthy patrons.

_____ _____ _____   10. Jim Walton, who was a great basketball player, now is a prominent coach.

_____ _____ _____   11. We walked carefully into the room that holds many kinds of snakes.

_____ _____ _____   12. Most of the desks that are in my classroom are marred with scratches.

_____ _____ _____   13. She admired my room that has been decorated recently.

_____ _____ _____   14. We met the man who invented Scrabble.

_____ _____ _____   15. All the boxes that are piled up in our yard will be used for toys for the poor.

_____ _____ _____   16. She learned to type on the keyboard of her new computer that her father gave her at graduation.

_____ _____ _____ 17. My little convertible, which I earned by working at Denny's, is my prize possession.

_____ _____ _____ 18. My brother fixed the door that was damaged by robbers.

_____ _____ _____ 19. Esther, who is an excellent speaker, will speak at our graduation.

_____ _____ _____ 20. We all enjoyed the skit that was given by the senior class.

_____ _____ _____ 21. We met Jody, who loves to entertain at birthday parties.

_____ _____ _____ 22. The essay that we have to write for our English class is due on Monday.

_____ _____ _____ 23. My brother works long hours in his photography shop that was a gift from his father.

_____ _____ _____ 24. Jane, who has a beautiful soprano voice, entertains her relatives and friends at concerts.

_____ _____ _____ 25. Stevie, who is the quarterback for our football team, played an exceptional game last night.

Modification

Modification refers to any word, phrase, or clause that modifies an antecedent. Modifiers are adjectives, apposition, participles, adjective clauses, and relative adverbs.

1. *Adjectives*

Adjectives modify nouns.

> *stale* bread

2. *Apposition*

Apposition refers to its antecedent giving more details.

> Jack, chief *commentator* for NBC tennis, was commended for his excellent reporting.

3. *Participle*

Participles are verbal adjectives always modifying a noun.

> Jan entered the arena, *belting* out the national anthem.

4. *Adjective clause*

Adjective clauses are introduced by a relative pronoun that takes the place of its antecedent, and are a part of the adjective clause.

> Elvis Presley, *who helped create rock music*, promoted it through many live performances.

5. *Relative adverbs*

Relative adverbs are also modifiers.

> There is a time *when* we cannot study.

Joining Sentences

Students' writing often suffers from a series of short sentences that could be joined by modification.

> Janet is an excellent violinist. She often gives concerts.
>
> *Jane, an excellent violinist, often gives concerts. (apposition)*
>
> *Jane, who is an excellent violinist, often gives concerts.* (adjective clause)

> Bob is the brightest boy in his class. He was elected student body president last month.
>
> *Bob, the brightest boy in his class, was elected student body president last month. (apposition)*
>
> *Bob, who was elected student body president last month, is the brightest boy in his class.* (adjective clause)
>
> *Bob, elected student body president last month, is the brightest boy in his class.* (participle)

Exercise 43

Directions: On a separate sheet of paper, combine the following sentences using modification. There can be more than one way to combine by modification.

1. Everyone in the class had a wonderful time at the graduation party. Janet's mother and her friends had spent hours planning it.

2. Leonardo da Vinci was born in 1452. He was born in Italy. He had great talent in art. His paintings are among the most famous in the world.

3. Robert Penn Warren is one of the most highly awarded writers in the history of the United States. He was America's first Poet Laureate. He won the Pulitzer Prize three times for fiction and twice for poetry.

4. In 1938, Warren became widely recognized in the academic field with his publication of *Understanding Poetry*. For a long time, this book changed the way poetry was taught and read.

5. Tom is my oldest brother. He goes to Adams High School. He is on the football team.

Unit 4
Noun Clauses

A **noun clause** is a dependent clause used like a noun.

Noun clauses often begin with the words *that, which, who, whom,* or *whose,* the same pronouns used to begin adjective or relative clauses. Noun clauses can also use variants of those words such as *whichever, whoever,* or *whomever.* Noun clauses may also begin with the words *when, where, whether, why, how, if, what,* or *whatever.* Many of these words can also be a part of the noun clause.

Introductory words in a noun clause can be **functional** or **nonfunctional**. The word has no function when it is not a part of the clause.

> I knew *that* I should not leave.

> She asked *whether* we should go.

Words are functional when they are part of the noun clause.

> No one knew *where* we were headed. (adverb)

> They did not tell us which car we should take. (adjective)

A noun clause has the same functions as a noun: subject, direct object, indirect object, subject complement, object of a preposition, and apposition.

1. *Subject*

> Whoever wrote the best essay won a trip to England.

In this sentence, the entire clause is the subject of the verb *won.*

When working with noun clauses, the main or independent clause may seem incomplete, but you must remember that the noun clause completes the main clause. In the above sentence, the noun clause subject completes the main clause *won a trip to England.*

> That he was unhappy over the outcome of the exam was evident to everyone.

That, the introductory word, has no function. The noun clause is used as the subject of the latter verb *was.*

Exercise 44

Directions: Underline the noun clause in the following sentences.
Example: <u>Whoever took my homework</u> will be sorry.

1. That Steve will succeed in his new job is almost assured.

2. Whoever finishes first will receive a prize.

3. What you do next depends on you.

4. Whatever way you go does not really matter.

5. Whether he will finish on time is debatable.

6. That Jim is a good student is evident by his work.

7. What Elsie did with the prize money was up to her.

8. Whoever finishes first must do the dishes.

9. When the storm will be over is hard to estimate.

10. That John is very clever was shown yesterday.

Directions: On a separate piece of paper, add noun clauses to the following predicates.

1. surprised us all
2. might be false
3. may leave early
4. makes no difference
5. could cause a problem

6. is true
7. is in our history book
8. made the teacher happy
9. must do the dishes
10. did not surprise his friends

2. *Direct object*

Noun clauses are used like direct objects or complements of a transitive verb when the entire clause answers the question *what*.

> Bob thought that we were too careful.

The noun clause is the direct object of *thought*. The main clause is *Bob thought*. The noun clause completes the main clause, and *that* has no function.

> We agreed that he is a great chairperson.
>
> We agreed that she would be elected.

These clauses answer the question *what*.

> He knew *who* locked the door. (subject)
>
> They told us *how* he would react. (adverb)
>
> Do you know *whose* car this is? (adjective)
>
> Do you know *whether* Jane will be there? (no function)
>
> No one knew *where* the keys were. (adverb)

Directions: Underline the noun clauses in the following sentences. Give the function of the introductory word. If it does not have a function, write *No*.

Example: <u>*No*</u>　We agreed <u>that the class needed a party</u>.

_____ 1.　No one in the class knew where the teacher put our papers.

_____ 2.　The teacher said that we would go on a field trip soon.

_____ 3.　Mollie said that she would be moving next semester.

_____ 4.　Bob asked which class would be dropped.

_____ 5.　We did not know how he would react to the announcement.

_____ 6.　We agreed that we would debate the issue tomorrow.

_____ 7.　The catalog lists which teacher will teach each course.

_____ 8.　We could not remember when the test would be given.

_____ 9.　We all wondered which book we would read next.

_____ 10.　We debated where we would hold the prom.

3. Indirect object

When the clause answers *to whom* or *from whom* something is given, the clause is the indirect object of the transitive verb. The indirect object comes between the transitive verb and the direct object.

His look of hatred gave whoever saw him a feeling of fear.

The main clause is *look gave feeling*. The noun clause is *(to) whoever saw him*.

Send whomever you want this pamphlet.

The main clause is *(you) send pamphlet*. The noun clause is *(to) whomever you want*.

main clause	noun clause, indirect object	direct object
The teacher gave	whoever wanted it	the answers
We sent	whoever was at the meeting	a copy of the speech

Remember that the subject of a clause is always in the nominative case.

Exercise 47

Directions: Fill in the blanks with either *whoever* or *whomever*.

Example: I will give   *whoever*   wrote this letter a subscription to our magazine.

1. We sent _____ was at the meeting this book.

2. Please give _____ you will meet our greetings.

3. I want to give _____ sent me the candy my sincerest thanks.

4. The committee sent _____ they thought worthy the basket of food.

5. The class chose _____ wrote the best speech their representative.

6. The principal will appoint_____ did the best job to represent the school at the convention.

7. Give _____ you want this book.

8. Out of his abundance, he gave _____ asked for it a substantial bonus.

9. We will send _____ they choose the final reports.

10. Please give _____ you choose a merit badge.

4. Subject complement (predicate nominative)

When a clause complements the subject following a linking verb, the clause is a noun clause.

The coach's problem is whether Jerry can play in the game tomorrow.

Problem and *whether Jerry can play in the game tomorrow* are the same, linked by *is*.

Her hope was that her brother would soon come home from Africa.

Hope and *brother would soon come home* are the same, linked by *was*.

My one desire was that I can go to college.

The news was that the game was postponed.

Directions: Underline the noun clauses in the following sentences.

Example: The fact could be <u>that John was lying</u>.

1. The rumor was that Joe was leaving the state.

2. My one desire is that I can go to Vassar.

3. The news was that our team had won the game.

4. The truth is that there can be no free day this semester.

5. The fact was that Jim failed both exams.

6. His purpose in holding the meeting was that there could be more group unity.

7. My only reason for my action was that the boys would be more respectful.

8. His desire could be that he wants to be president.

9. Jerry's hope is that he can become a journalist.

10. The news is that school will be closed on Friday.

5. *Object of preposition*

Noun clauses can also be used as the object of prepositions.

> Use this material for whatever purpose you choose.

The object of the preposition *for* is the noun clause *whatever purpose you choose.*

> He talks to whoever sits beside him.
> We sent the package to whoever asked for it.
> This material is for the project you must complete.

Directions: Underline the noun clauses in the following sentences.

Example: We had an idea of <u>what she wanted</u>.

1. Just leave the message with whoever answers the door.

2. We argued about where we would eat.

3. They wondered about how they would cross the desert.

4. My friend was angered by whoever rang the doorbell.

5. We are seldom pleased with what they tell us.

6. Jerry had no idea of why he sent that message.

7. Give this pencil to whoever bought it.

8. We were overjoyed by what he told us.

9. These papers are for the work you must do.

10. Send these reports to whoever requested them.

6. *Apposition*

A clause used in apposition is a noun clause.

> The fact that he cannot possibly win the election is hard for him to accept.

What is the fact? *that he cannot possibly win the election*

The noun clause is in apposition to the fact, telling what the fact is.

> The teacher's dilemma, what he should do with the assignments, required thoughtful planning.

What is the dilemma? *what he should do with the assignments*

The noun clause in apposition tells what the dilemma is.

Exercise 50

Directions: Underline the noun clauses in the following sentences.

Example: Please send <u>whoever wrote for it</u> this material.

1. Send whoever asked for it this money.

2. That you can be very slow sometimes is evident.

3. Whoever works the hardest will receive the prize.

4. I cannot understand why he refused to attend the workshops.

5. We all agreed that we would not meet for another month.

6. The argument started over who would take Jerry to school.

7. That we won the game did not surprise us.

8. The question is whether we can play in the tournament.

9. What you choose to do is your decision.

10. The decision that we should all remain in the room angered us.

11. Your grade on the final exam will determine whether you will pass the course.

12. My father's worry, how he can get a job, affected the entire house.

13. We will agree with whoever gives the best advice.

14. The most difficult question was whether the entire time should be devoted to a single topic.

15. They will select whoever puts in an application.

16. She asked whether I would help her write the paper.

17. She said that Jerry and she would leave later.

18. That the paper was poorly written was certainly evident.

19. My brother's favorite excuse is that the dog tore up his homework.

20. That my little sister was selected the best player pleased my father.

That *Introduces Adverb, Adjective, and Noun Clauses*

1. *Adverb clauses*

That in an adverb clause generally answers the question *why*. *So that* or *in order that* can be added. *That* never takes the place of a noun in an adverb clause.

> Tom works hard so that he will get a raise.

The adverb clause *so that he will get a raise* answers the question *why*.

> He is always careful so that he doesn't have an accident.

The adverb clause *so that he doesn't have an accident* modifies the adjective *careful*, explaining why he is careful.

2. *Relative or adjective clause*

That in a relative clause takes the place of its antecedent and is always a part of the relative clause.

> We read the short story that you wrote.

The antecedent of *that* is *story*, and it is used as the direct object of *wrote*.

> I wrote the letter that he sent to the principal.

The antecedent of *that* is *letter*, and it is used as the direct object of *sent*.

3. *Noun clause*

That in a noun clause merely introduces the clause. It is never a part of the clause; it is never functional.

> She said that she will go to the mall with us.

In this sentence, *that* introduces the noun clause but has no function in the clause.

> We all agreed that she was the best actress.

Noun Clauses in Apposition and Adjective Clauses

Sometimes students confuse noun clauses in apposition with adjective (relative) clauses. *That* in a noun clause is never functional, while *that* in a relative clause is a part of the relative clause.

> I read the news that he had an accident.

That is not functional. *He had an accident* states what the news is.

> I read the news that was in the paper.

That is functional and is the subject of the relative clause. It states where the news is.

> The report that there was an earthquake alarmed my mother. (noun clause)

> The report that was in the paper explained the situation. (adjective clause)

Exercise 51

Directions: Write *N* if the dependent clause is a noun clause or *A* if it is an adjective clause.

Example: <u>*A*</u>   The schedule that was in the school paper was incorrect.

_____1.   The news that the game was forfeited did not reach us until evening.

_____2.   The report that a second plane had crashed brought much grief.

_____3.   The news that was in *Newsweek* was exaggerated.

_____4.   The news that there was an earthquake in Japan worried everyone.

_____5. We all understood the remarks that the teacher made.

_____6. The statement that more doctors were needed in our hospitals influenced me to become a doctor.

_____7. Did you read the report that was in the *Banner*?

_____8. Did you read the report that our team must travel to Oregon?

_____9. The article that was on the bulletin board is false.

_____10. Did you understand the rules that the principal published?

Review

There are three kinds of dependent clauses: adverb, adjective (relative), and noun clauses.

Adverb Clauses

An adverb clause is introduced by a subordinate conjunction. A subordinate conjunction makes an independent clause dependent. Adverb clauses answer the questions *when, where, why, how, to what extent, in what manner,* or *under what conditions.*

Elliptical Clauses

Elliptical clauses are adverb clauses generally introduced by the subordinate conjunctions *than, as, since, while,* or *when.* They are elliptical because words are omitted.

Punctuation

When the adverb clause comes first (periodic), use commas. When the adverb clause comes last (loose), do not use commas except for clarity.

Adjective (Relative) Clauses

An adjective clause is introduced by a relative pronoun or adjective: *who, whom, which, what, that,* or *whose.* The relative pronoun is always a part of the relative clause and refers to its antecedent.

Punctuation

If the relative clause is restrictive, do not use commas. If the relative clause is not restrictive, use commas.

Noun Clauses

A noun clause always completes a main clause. The noun clause is the subject, direct object, indirect object, object of a preposition, or apposition to the main clause.

Punctuation

No punctuation needed.

Directions: Write *A* for adverb clause, *R* for relative clause, or *N* for noun clause.

_____1. Tom, *who works for my father,* received a raise last week.

_____2. *After you finish that assignment,* put it on my desk.

_____3. The news *that was in the paper* shocked everyone.

_____4. I returned the book *where you left it.*

_____5. I read the article *that he wrote for the bulletin.*

_____6. We read the notice *that a storm is on the way.*

_____7. *That the fruit is overripe* is very evident.

_____8. The fact *that he disqualified himself from the competition* was his own problem.

_____9. Mary works harder and faster *than Meg.*

_____10. *Since we visit the convalescent home each Saturday,* we have learned to love the residents there.

_____11. The girl *of whom I spoke* is now chairperson of the food committee.

_____12. *After they had fought in the war,* the boys were glad to come home.

_____13. *As long as Ted starts early,* he will arrive on time.

_____14. *While visiting my cousin in Arizona,* we toured the Grand Canyon.

_____15. We thought *that her brother was overzealous.*

_____16. Jean works after school *so that she has spending money.*

_____17. Donna sounds *as if she has caught a cold.*

_____18. Greg, *who is an excellent diver,* won two gold medals.

_____19. Give help *where it is needed.*

_____20. The coat *that I want* is very expensive.

_____21. Any complaints will be handled by *whoever is in charge.*

_____22. Everyone prays *that Bob will be better soon.*

_____23. The grocer will give *whoever shops early* a cherry pie.

_____24. Jess, the little dog *that was given to me for my birthday,* wandered away from my home.

_____25. *Before you sign the contract,* have your attorney check it.

_____26. We heard *that Jean won first prize* in the essay contest.

_____27. The rain *that fell last night* was like a drop in a bucket.

_____28. The news *that the Christmas vacation would be extended* thrilled the entire student body.

_____29. *If it rains,* we will leave early.

_____30. This is the hour *when the contract was signed.*

Exercise 53

Directions: Using the sentences from **Exercise 52**, write out the relative pronouns for relative clauses, the subordinate conjunction for adverb clauses, or the use of the noun clause.

Exercise 54

Directions: On notebook paper, write out sentences that use dependent clauses from a novel or short story from your literature book. Try to find different kinds of dependent clauses.

Exercise 55

Directions: Write *A* for adverb clause, *R* for relative clause, or *N* for noun clause.

_____1. lady *who lives next door*

_____2. *after he left for the store*

_____3. report *that he died*

_____4. news *that was on the bulletin board*

_____5. *since he is leaving for Japan*

_____6. John, *whose bike was stolen,*

_____7. *because she hesitated in answering his letter*

_____8. said *that he would come later*

_____9. *if you continue to improve*

_____10. time *when she would come*

_____11. report *that the meeting would be held on Friday*

_____12. *although Mary failed the final examination*

_____13. pencil *that was found*

_____14. Jeff, *whose house was robbed,*

_____15. worked hard *that he might earn a scholarship*

_____16. agreed *that he would join the party*

_____17. of *why she left so early*

_____18. is *that he is not dedicated*

_____19. report *that I handed in*

_____20. *who teaches my brother*

_____21. roof *that was fixed*

_____22. bike *that was damaged*

_____23. *after she sang the song*

_____24. news *that he lost his wallet*

_____25. news *that was in the paper*

_____26. agreed *that she was a good reader.*

_____27. yard *that was needed*

_____28. *as long as he could stand it*

_____29. *if he finds our car*

_____30. friend *who came yesterday*

_____31. to *whoever is in the room*

_____32. the question of *when he entered the room*

_____33. was *that they are winning*

_____34. knew *who broke the window*

_____35. room *that he painted*

_____36. notice *that he read*

_____37. news *that he will graduate*

_____38. *that he is an excellent student*

_____39. *before you hand in that assignment*

_____40. said *that he is leaving*

_____41. *although he is leaving*

_____42. could be *that he is the teacher*

_____43. cousin *who visited my aunt* in Kentucky

_____44. *while you are working on that puzzle*

_____45. to *whoever wants it*

_____46. knew *that Molly was arriving*

_____47. of *why he is moving*

_____48. garden *that I planted*

_____49. report *that Ed won the contest*

_____50. argued *that he was in the right*

Who *and* Whom

The use of *who* or *whom* is determined by the structure of the sentence or clause. See Unit 5 for definitions of sentence structures.

Who is always in the nominative case: subject, subject complement.

Whom is always in the objective case: direct object, indirect object, object of the preposition.

Whoever and *whomever* are used like *who* and *whom*.

> Mary is the senior who received the award for excellence.

Who is the subject of the adjective clause.

> Tom is the soldier whom I met at Camp Pendleton.

Whom is the direct object of *met* in the relative clause.

Simple

Of whom did you speak? You did speak of whom?

To whom did you give the paper? You gave the paper to whom?

Who took my book?

Complex with Relative Pronouns

The boy of whom you spoke came from Italy.

The teacher to whom you gave the paper will be leaving next month.

The girl who took my book did it by mistake.

Noun Clauses

Noun clauses complete the main clause and have their own structure.

Please give this library card to whoever left it in the library.

Whoever is the subject of the noun clause. The noun clause *whoever left it in the library* is the object of the preposition *to.*

Give whomever you want this book.

The noun clause *whomever you want* is the indirect object. The *whomever* is the direct object of *want.*

The subject of a clause is always in the nominative case.

Give this book to whoever is in the room.

The entire noun clause *whoever is in the room* is the object of the preposition *to. Whoever* is the subject of the clause and must be in the nominative case.

To whom will you send the money?

In this sentence *whom* is the object of the preposition *to.*

Please give the money to whoever calls for it.

Whoever is not the object of *to,* the entire clause *whoever calls for it* is the object of *to. Whoever* is in the nominative case—subject of the noun clause.

Who do you think sent me this letter? (Who sent me this letter?)

Whom do you think they have appointed? (They have appointed whom?)

Who do you suppose wrote that report? (Who wrote that report?)

Whom do you suppose they will give it to? (They will give it to whom?)

Please give this book to whoever walks in the room.

Please give this book to whomever you choose.

Exercise 56

Directions: Write the letter of the correct answer.

Example: *B*   (A. Who B. Whom) do you think she phoned?

_____1. Brian is a soldier (A. who B. whom) everyone likes.

_____2. Send (A. whoever B. whomever) you want this bouquet.

_____3. Do you know to (A. who B. whom) they gave this letter?

_____4. Give the letter to (A. whoever B. whomever) knows the sender.

_____5. (A. Whoever B. Whomever) enters the room first should clean the blackboards.

_____6. Chalk and crayons are available for (A. whoever B. whomever) requests them.

_____7. Jill, (A. who B. whom) you saw at the show last evening, prefers pop-corn to candy.

_____8. Mrs. Gross is the chaperone (A. who B. whom) everyone likes.

_____9. (A. Who B. Whom) plans the activities is the most important person.

_____10. (A. Who B. Whom) do you think the teacher will choose?

_____11. Please send this report to (A. whoever B. whomever) has asked for it.

_____12. (A. Who B. Whom) the students choose for their president is an impor-tant decision.

_____13. We met the author about (A. who B. whom) we had read.

_____14. Loretta thanked the teacher from (A. who B. whom) she had received so much help.

_____15. The policeman knows (A. who B. whom) we want.

_____16. They gave the ticket to the man (A. who B. whom) had left his car in the wrong parking lot.

_____17. We all knew (A. who B. whom) the culprit was.

_____18. (A. Who B. Whom) do you suppose will receive the athletic award at the end of the year?

_____19. Please thank the boys (A. who B. whom) cleaned up the yard.

_____20. She is the teacher (A. who B. whom) I most admire.

_____21. This is the actress about (A. who B. whom) I told you.

_____22. The girl (A. who B. whom) you met last week is a cousin of mine.

_____23. Please take these roses to my aunt (A. who B. whom) is in Memorial County Hospital.

_____24. Do you know (A. who B. whom) is concerned with our cause?

_____25. Would you please give this book to (A. whoever B. whomever) is at the desk in the library?

_____26. Do you know (A. who B. whom) advertised for the position?

_____27. Helen is the only one (A. who B. whom) has never lost a game of checkers.

_____28. (A. Who B. Whom) did the Lakers beat last night?

_____29. With (A. who B. whom) are you going to the dance?

_____30. To (A. who B. whom) do you think you are speaking?

_____31. We had no idea of (A. who B. whom) he was representing.

_____32. (A. Who B. Whom) do you think they want?

_____33. Give my best regards to (A. whoever B. whomever) is at the reception.

_____34. The class voted for (A. who B. whom) they wanted for treasurer.

_____35. The money is for (A. who B. whom)?

_____36. (A. Who B. Whom) will be going to a junior college?

Exercise 57

Directions: Underline the noun clause and indicate its function in the sentence by writing *S* for subject, *DO* for direct object, *IO* for indirect object, *OP* for object of preposition, *C* for subject complement, or *A* for apposition.

Example: _A_   Jane, <u>who made the basketball team</u>, is a sophomore.

_____1. That she is impossible to please makes it difficult to live with her.

_____2. We did not know where she put all the papers.

_____3. The teacher said that we should relax this weekend.

_____4. Please give this note to whoever answers the door.

_____5. The truth is that she did not study.

_____6. Please give whoever answers the door this note.

_____7. We have no idea of why she is moving to Canada.

_____8. That he would make a good president is debatable.

_____9. Whoever needs help on the project should ask me.

_____10. We agreed that we would all meet in the gym.

_____11. His recommendation that we should lay off at least a hundred employees brought us real grief.

_____12. That this will cause a terrible hardship is inevitable.

_____13. The article that Japan needs help surprised no one.

_____14. Lori said that she will graduate from Purdue University in two years.

_____15. We would like to know when he took the state boards.

_____16. That Lois is a good basketball player cannot be denied.

_____17. The fact is that Lois will receive a college scholarship.

_____18. The report that the earthquake registered 7.4 shocked me.

_____19. He demanded to know who set off the alarm.

_____20. Mildred said that she had never watched a boxing match.

Indirect and Direct Discourse

Because all indirect and direct discourse are noun clauses, the study of quotations is included in this section.

Indirect discourse means that the words of the speaker are given but not quoted exactly, so quotation marks are not used.

> Pete said that he plans to go to Ireland this summer.

> Jane announced that the dance has been canceled.

Direct discourse means that the words of the speaker are given exactly. When a person's exact words or thoughts are stated, quotation marks must be used.

Rules Governing Quotation Marks

1. *Main clause followed by a noun clause*

> The principal explained, "Your report cards will be mailed next week."

Read this aloud as follows: The principal explained, comma, open quote, capital Y, Your report cards will be mailed next week, period, close quote.

> The coach declared, "No one can play on Saturday who has not practiced."

Read: The coach declared, comma, open quote, capital N, No one can play on Saturday who has not practiced, period, close quote.

Periods and commas are always inside the quotation marks. This rule never changes.

2. *Noun clause followed by main clause*

> "I would love to play volleyball," my little sister announced.

Read: Open quote, capital I, I would love to play volleyball, comma, close quote, my little sister declared, period.

> "Tom should win the speech tournament," the teacher said.

Read: Open quote, capital T, Tom should win the speech tournament, comma, close quote, the teacher said, period.

3. *Main clause followed by a noun clause that is a question*

> Pete asked, "Where did you put my books?"

Read: Pete asked, comma, open quote, capital W, Where did you put my books, question mark, close quote.

> My mother asked, "Why are you home so early?"

Read: My mother asked, comma, open quote, capital W, Why are you home so early, question mark, close quote.

4. *The noun clause question followed by the main clause*

> "Did you see my skates anywhere?" my brother asked.

Read: Open quote, capital D, Did you see my skates anywhere, question mark. close quote, my brother asked, period.

> "What happened to you?" my friend asked.

Read: Open quote, capital W, What happened to you, question mark, close quote, my friend asked, period.

Directions: Rewrite the following sentences correctly.

Example: My mother said finish your beets *My mother said, "Finish your beets."*

1. I asked how do you know she will be on time

2. The boy cried I spent three hours on homework last night

3. Why did you leave so quickly he asked

4. Are you going to ask Ted to the picnic Mary asked

5. I really like our school jacket I said

6. The coach said we are coming home the victors on Friday night

7. Where are you going this summer I asked

8. Have you seen that movie before James inquired

9. You must keep your eye on the ball the coach instructed

10. Don't forget my anniversary my mother announced one morning

5. *Broken quote, one sentence*

"When we get to the dance this evening," my date said, "we will first get our pictures taken."

Read: Open quote, capital W, When we get to the dance this evening, comma, close quote, my date said, comma, open quote, we will first get our pictures taken, period, close quote.

"Where," he asked, "did you put my jacket?"

Read: Open quote, capital W, Where, comma, close quote, he asked, comma, open quote, did you put my jacket, question mark, close quote.

Exercise 59

Directions: Punctuate the following sentences correctly.

Example: Do I turn here I asked or at the next light? *"Do I turn here," I asked, "or at the next light?"*

1. It is not true she replied that I did his homework for him.

2. When you visit me in Texas my cousin wrote be sure to bring your hat and boots.

3. We will be closing the park for a week the ranger said in order to make the necessary repairs.

4. I'll have to ask the teacher Carla answered because I can't give you permission to leave.

5. If we can win this game Jeff said then we can be the champions of Arkansas.

6. If I can get to the box office this morning Lori promised I'll get the tickets.

7. When you finish the dishes my mother said you may visit your friend.

8. After you see the movie Pete replied meet us at Carnation Parlor.

9. Look up the material in the encyclopedia the professor said if you want to have a documented term paper.

10. I fail to see Jason said how you wrote that paper so quickly.

6. *Broken quote, more than one sentence*

> "We will leave early tomorrow morning," the camp counselor said. "We want to be at Big Bear by 10:00 A.M."

Read: Open quote, capital W, We will leave tomorrow morning, comma, close quote, the camp counselor said, period, open quote, capital W, We want to be at Big Bear by 10:00 A.M., period, close quote.

> "If you check the place where you found the jewelry," my father said, "you will discover other evidence of robbery. It is evident that there was foul play here."

Read: Open quote, capital I, If you check the place where you found the jewelry, comma, close quote, my father said, comma, open quote, you will discover other evidence of robbery, period, capital I, It is evident that there was foul play here, period, close quote.

Exercise 60

Directions: Punctuate these sentences correctly.

Example: Turn now she answered and go two blocks turn left at the blue house
"Turn now," she answered, "and go two blocks. Turn left at the blue house."

1. I will never forget Bob said the evening we camped out at Lake Mountains it was the worst evening of my life

2. I wish I had studied harder Jean moaned I know I am going to fail this test

3. If you leave immediately I said you will be on time for class you don't want to be late a third time

4. I believe said Ted that we can reach the campsite by 2:00 A.M. we could get there sooner if we would stop dawdling

5. Tom I asked may I borrow your book for an hour I will put it on your desk when I am finished

7. *Quotations with question marks*

When the quotation is a question, the question mark is inside the quotation mark.

> My little brother asked, "Will you take me to Disneyland?"
> Bob asked, "Where are my baseball gloves?"

When the quotation is not a question, the quotation mark comes before the question mark.

> Did the coach say, "There will be no baseball practice tonight"?
> Have you ever read the short story "The Most Dangerous Game"?

8. *Quotation marks with exclamation marks*

Exclamation marks are handled the same way as question marks.

When the quotation is an exclamation, the exclamation mark is inside the quotation marks.

> "Leave her alone!" he shouted.

> "Help! Help!" he cried.

When the quotation is not an exclamation, the quotation mark comes before the exclamation mark. Generally, the quote is an exclamation.

> I could hardly believe he said "Everyone can go home"!

9. *Semicolons and colons with quotation marks*

Semicolons and colons are placed outside the closing quotation mark. There are no exceptions to this rule.

> Mary said, "I usually dislike science fiction"; however, she came to the movies with us anyway.

> Our British Literature class only reads works described as "classics": Shakespeare's plays, Dickens's novels, and Donne's essays.

10. *Quotation within a quotation*

When there is a quoted statement within another quotation, use a single quotation mark for the quotation within the quotation.

> "When," my brother shouted, "did you ever hear Tom say, 'I refuse to play soccer'?"

In this example, the question mark goes outside the single quote because that quote is not a question.

> The teacher said, "For the next class, everyone must read the poem 'Sea Fever.'"

The single quotation mark goes outside the period in the same way a double quotation mark does.

11. *Quotation marks with dialogue*

Each time a new speaker is quoted, begin a new paragraph.

> "I told you last week that I needed the book," Jeff complained. "Why didn't you finish your paper then?"

> "Well, I kept getting interrupted," Mike explained.

> "That's no excuse," Jeff whined.

12. *Quotation marks with long quotations*

In academic situations, if more than a full sentence from the original source is quoted, or if the material would take more than four written lines, it should be indented and single-spaced, with no quotation marks.

> Various theories have been proposed over the years. Johnson's is the most accepted, but experts are still deliberating. Lewis's report lists some of the nagging doubts.

> > The circumstances, as generally agreed upon by respected investigators, dictate that he could not possibly have seen the perpetrator. In that case, how can his claim of eyewitness evidence stand in a court of law? Several other discrepancies remain, not the least of which is how the camel appeared on the roof.

However, in most other circumstances, it is acceptable to put quotation marks only at the beginning of each paragraph of a lengthy quotation and have closing quotation marks at the end of the final paragraph.

> Sally Smythe laughed at the suggestion that she is a role model for women in sports.
>
> "I didn't have any idea," she explained, "that what I was doing was considered a first step for women. I only wanted to play ball.
>
> "I didn't care about making statements on gender issues. I was twelve, for crying out loud.
>
> "I think that when you are in a situation, it's hard for you to see beyond those present circumstances, and to consider what people will label you in the future. That's probably why all this is so surprising to me."

Review

Periods and commas are always inside the quotation mark. No exceptions.

When the quote is a question or exclamation, the quotation mark is outside of the question or exclamation mark. When the quote is not a question or an exclamation, the quotation mark is inside the question or exclamation mark. It seldom happens that an exclamation is not a quote.

Always place semicolons and colons outside the quotation mark. This rule never changes.

In dialogue, begin a new paragraph with each change of speaker.

For quotations longer than a paragraph, put quotation marks at the beginning of each paragraph and at the end of the final paragraph.

Exercise 61

Directions: Punctuate the following sentences.

1. Where did you put the balloons for the party I asked

2. The boy screamed the boy in that blue convertible stole my jacket

3. Did the speech teacher say meet near the gym at 8:00 A.M

4. Were you planning to leave later I asked

5. Has everyone bought tickets for the Lakers game Friday night he asked

6. Did you see my sister in the cafeteria I asked.

7. We were certainly not aware the cop replied that the spring vacation had already started give us the exact dates so that we can check

8. Are you planning Sharon asked to go to the Friendship Dance on Saturday night it is sponsored by the freshman class

9. Did you see his bike at the park Paul asked

10. Did you read the sign that said boys not allowed

11. Nothing could make her feel better I said she was really upset

12. My mechanic said your engine needs work you better let us keep your car overnight

13. My uncle called my house this morning and said we have a beautiful baby girl

14. Did you hear the principal say school will be canceled for two days

15. The student asked did you see my math book lying around anywhere

16. The judge said there is a law that says no drunk driving

17. My brother ran into the house and enthusiastically announced I made 100% on my semester math exam

18. Did you read the notice that said if you are going to Europe this summer please turn in your registration form by Friday of this week

19. The game was really a close one he said it took until the last four seconds to win

20. Did Miss Jones really say I will not accept late papers

21. My teacher asked who spilled this ink

22. The operator announced a world record was set in the last race

23. If you decide to go with us please let us know by tomorrow

24. Nothing, he said, can atone for the loss of my little brother

25. Didn't you read the notice that said no smoking

Exercise 62

Directions: Rewrite the following conversation on notebook paper. Punctuate correctly.

Hey Jim are you planning to come to the game with us tonight we are playing the Bengals and they're a tough team to beat sorry Greg I can't I have to go to the library and work on my history paper if I don't bring my grades up Mom says I can kiss the car goodbye have you started yours yet no not really but the league championship might depend on this game so I really want to go I'll get my paper done on the weekend it's due this Monday right I think so are you going to get pizza after the game no we're thinking of McDonald's maybe I can meet you there later I should have all of my research done by then yes you'll be ready for a study break we'll be at the one on East Avenue what time will you and the others be there we should definitely be there by ten okay I'll see you then Greg bye

Nouns, gerunds, and noun clauses all are used the same way nouns are used.

1. *Subject*

Nouns, gerunds, and noun clauses can be used as subjects.

2. *Complements*

Nouns, gerunds, and noun clauses can be used as complements of the subject after linking verbs, as complements of a transitive verb, as indirect complements of a transitive verb, as complements of a preposition, or in apposition to the subject.

Exercise 63

Part A.

Directions: On a separate piece of paper, write original sentences using the following suggestions.

Example: gerund subject   *Swimming can be a healthful sport.*

1. gerund direct object
2. noun clause direct object
3. gerund indirect object
4. noun clause indirect object
5. gerund subject complement
6. noun clause subject complement
7. gerund apposition
8. noun clause apposition
9. gerund subject
10. noun clause subject
11. gerund object of a preposition
12. noun clause object of a preposition

Part B.

Directions: Punctuate the following sentences correctly.

13. Jerry said I am going camping on Saturday do you want to come with me

14. Where she asked did you put the paper I gave you to read

15. Did you study the one-act play Trifles

16. While the weather is warm Joan said let's go to the beach I am dying to feel those fresh sea breezes

17. Did you finish your term paper I asked I stayed up all night to finish mine

18. Did you hear him say there is nothing we can do about the situation

19. Next week our philosophy teacher said we will discuss *Carpe diem* seize the day

20. Out of my way yelled Melissa I'm late

Unit 5

Compound Sentences

A **compound sentence** has two or more independent clauses.

> Misers get up early in the morning, and burglars stay up the night before.

Both of these clauses are independent; neither clause is dependent on the other.

> Joe left early, but we waited for the refreshments.

Both of these clauses have equal value. The **coordinate conjunction** *but* joins them. There is no possibility of reducing one of these independent clauses; a subordinate conjunction would change the meaning.

Coordinate Conjunctions

The coordinate conjunctions are *and, but, or, nor, for,* and *yet.* These conjunctions are called coordinate because they join independent clauses.

> He speaks fluently, but his brother can hardly speak at all.

Note that the coordinate conjunction keeps the clauses independent.

> Ted has to work hard on his Spanish, but Jack seldom needs to study.

> Everyone took a list and we began the scavenger hunt.

> They plan to go to the game or they will go to the party.

In each of the sentences, the pattern is independent clause, coordinate conjunction, independent clause.

Coordination

Coordination is joining independent words, phrases, and clauses. As opposed to subordination, coordination means that the words, phrases, and clauses are equal.

The coordinate conjunctions are *and, but, or, nor, for,* and *yet.*

1. Coordinate conjunctions often join compound subjects and compound predicates.

> Jane and Mary will attend the concert this evening.

> Debbie put her books on her desk and left the room.

2. Coordinate conjunctions join coordinate adjectives.

Coordinate adjectives modify a noun equally. To know whether the adjectives are coordinate, put the word *and* between them. Another way is to reverse the order. If the meaning does not change, they are coordinate.

> A large, (and) cumbersome, (and) angry elephant stood defiantly outside the ring. (coordinate adjectives)

> For her anniversary, my mother received fifty red roses.

Reversing the order to *red fifty roses* changes the meaning, so the adjectives are not coordinate.

3. Any kind of phrase can be joined with coordinate conjunctions.

> Swimming and bicycling are my favorite sports. (compound gerunds)
>
> She walked along the beach and into the water. (compound prepositional phrase)
>
> Lifting his bike and straightening the wheel, Jack was able to ride home. (compound participles)
>
> Mary likes to read, to play tennis, and to swim. (compound infinitives)

4. Coordinate conjunctions are used to join subordinate clauses.

> Because Molly finished her term paper, and because she has always done her homework, she will be permitted to join the golf squad this year. (compound adverb clauses)
>
> If you want to be admired, if you want to be popular, if you want to be successful, and if you want to make it in the corporate world, use this soap. (compound subordinate clauses)

5. Coordinate conjunctions join independent clauses.

> Everyone attended the class play, but very few enjoyed it.
>
> Alice was the daughter of the governor of the state, and she often bragged about her father.

Uses of But, And

The coordinate conjunction *but* changes the direction of the sentence.

> My brother loves sailing, but his classes keep him away from the water.
>
> Suddenly the bell rang for the end of the period, but several students had not finished the exam.

The coordinate conjunction *and* keeps the sentence moving forward.

> My brother loves sailing, and he often takes his friends with him.
>
> September came and school began.

Errors in the Use of Compound Sentences

Compound sentences should be used sparingly, and only when it is impossible to use a complex sentence.

1. Avoid excessive coordination

Remember that it is better to subordinate than coordinate. Excessive coordination is sometimes a problem for beginning writers who seldom subordinate because they see everything as equal, as in the following example.

> My mother took me and my brother shopping yesterday and first we went to a department store and bought me a dress and my brother a shirt and then we went and got something to eat and then we went to the movies and then we came home.

2. Avoid connecting unrelated ideas.

Unrelated ideas always must be separated. The idea expressed in the first clause must be carried over into the second, unlike the following sentence.

> Everyone at the time of the earthquake was terribly frightened, and my brother recalled the first earthquake he ever experienced.

3. Avoid unclear coordination.

The coordinate conjunction must link the clauses clearly.

> We tried to avoid the accident, yet we were unsuccessful.

Yet does not link the ideas clearly.

> Better: We tried to avoid the accident, *but* we were unsuccessful.

Weak coordination can often be improved by subordination.

> We attended the rally for peace, and we realized the dedication of the participants. (weak coordination)

> When we attended the rally for peace, we realized the dedication of the participants. (subordination makes a clearer sentence)

> We all enjoyed the show, and we decided to go again on the following day. (weak coordination)

> We all enjoyed the show, so we decided to go again on the following day. (subordination)

> Bill won the art contest last month, and he was given a scholarship for one year. (clauses not of equal value)

> Because Bill won the art contest last month, he was given a scholarship for one year. (subordination)

Conjunctive Adverbs

A **conjunctive adverb** is used to clarify the relationship between clauses of equal weight in a sentence. They are often used transitionally. The conjunctive adverbs used most frequently are *besides, furthermore, moreover, however, nevertheless, still, consequently, therefore, equally, likewise, similarly,* and *thus.*

Conjunctive adverbs are usually stronger and more precise than coordinating conjunctions.

> We were disappointed at the loss of the game, and we vowed to win the following year.

> We were disappointed at the loss of the game; however, we vowed to win the following year.

Exercise 64

Directions: Underline the conjunctive adverb in the following sentences.

Example: She submitted several poems and stories for consideration; <u>however</u>, the literary magazine only printed one.

1. I couldn't solve the problem; consequently, I had to ask for help.

2. Paul is a great athlete; moreover, he is an excellent student.

3. John injured his leg at basketball practice; therefore, he will not play tomorrow.

4. Fingerprints have helped to convict many guilty people; likewise, they have helped free many innocent people.

5. Each person's fingerprints are unique; similarly, each gun fires bullets with unique grooves.

Punctuation of Compound Sentences

1. *Comma with coordinate conjunctions*

Whenever a coordinate conjunction joins independent clauses, use a comma.

> Everybody left early, but I had to wait for my mother.

> They closed the dance at 11:00 P.M., and we all had to leave.

Do not use commas when joining compound predicates or dependent clauses with coordinate conjunctions.

> Bob ran into the house and grabbed his sweater. (compound predicate)

> I will take Algebra II or trigonometry next year. (compound object)

2. *Semicolons between independent clauses*

Use semicolons when the coordinate conjunction is omitted.

> Most of the class enjoyed the opera; a few detested it. (coordinate conjunction *but* is omitted)

Use semicolons when one or both clauses contain commas.

> American television broadcasts almost twenty-four hours a day; but British television, on the other hand, broadcasts about eighteen hours.

3. *Semicolons with conjunctive adverbs*

Conjunctive adverbs do not join clauses. They are generally used transitionally. Only coordinate conjunctions or semicolons can join clauses.

> We decided to hold a study session for the final exam, but two did not show up. (comma with coordinate conjunction)

> We decided to hold a study session for the final exam; however, two did not show up. (semicolon because the coordinate conjunction is missing)

> We decided to hold a study session for the final exam; two did not show up. (semicolon because the coordinate conjunction is missing)

When a semicolon or period precedes a conjunctive adverb, the conjunctive adverb is followed by a comma.

Exercise 65

Directions: On a separate piece of paper, write five original sentences using conjunctive adverbs. Punctuate correctly.

Exercise 66

Directions: On a separate piece of paper, supply conjunctive adverbs for the following sentences. Punctuate correctly.

Example: Karen had the flu. She played in the game last night.
> *Karen had the flu; nevertheless, she played in the game last night.*

1. Her plane was delayed in Missouri. It arrived two hours late.
2. Fewer people could afford new cars this year. There was less profit for the automobile industry.
3. My sister has a beautiful voice. She is often asked to sing at concerts.
4. John has received too many demerits. He cannot play football on Saturday night.
5. Mary was injured in an automobile accident. She cannot try out for cheerleading.
6. Joe practices ice skating four hours each day. He is an excellent skater.

7. We chose to go swimming. They wanted to go hiking.

8. It started to rain. The picnic had to be canceled.

9. Jerry flunked his math exam. He will have to get a tutor.

10. No one understood the teacher's instructions. We all had to stay after school.

Comma Splices

A **comma splice** occurs when two independent clauses are joined with a comma instead of a semicolon.

> We did not have school today, there is a faculty meeting.

This is incorrect, because the two independent clauses are joined with a comma but no coordinate conjunction.

> We did not have school today; there is a faculty meeting. (correct)
>
> John is a good student, he will pass the exam easily. (incorrect)
>
> John is a good student; he will pass the exam easily. (correct)
>
> John is a good student, and he will pass the exam easily. (correct)

Exercise 67

Directions: Punctuate the following sentences correctly.

Example: It is almost dinner time, we can't get there and back in time. *It is almost dinner time; we can't get there and back in time.*

1. Our team played hard, we lost by ten points.

2. I wasn't frightened by the wolf, I was terrified.

3. Order your tickets early, you might not get one.

4. Proceed quickly to the gym, we want to start immediately.

5. Terry wrote several letters to the editor, she never received an answer.

6. I could hardly wait to swim, the water looked so inviting.

7. We were all there for the party, Jack came an hour late.

8. The cookies were in the pantry, nobody looked there.

9. Hurry and greet the visitors, we can't keep them waiting.

10. My car is old, it still runs well.

Express Coordinate Ideas in Similar Form

Parallel construction requires that similar expressions in content and function be outwardly similar. This likeness of form enables the reader to recognize the likeness of content and function.

> I enjoy riding, singing, and swimming. (gerunds)
>
> That he was able to capture the attention of his audience, that he was able to inspire them to action, and that he was able to lead them constructively made Churchill a powerful leader for the English people during World War I. (noun clauses)

Parallel construction will be studied more thoroughly in Unit 6.

Correlative Conjunctions

Correlative conjunctions connect two ideas and are used in pairs to join words, phrases, and clauses that are parallel in form. The correlative conjunctions are

> both . . . and . . .
> either . . . or . . .
> neither . . . nor . . .
> not only . . . but also . . .
> whether . . . or . . .

The conjunctions are placed immediately before the parallel items. To be used correctly, the second correlative must be followed by a construction that is parallel to the first.

> Both my brother and my cousin have the measles.

Brother and *cousin* are of equal value. The correlative conjunction *both . . . and* makes the relationship clearer and stronger.

> Either you do the assignment or you forfeit the trip to Hawaii.

The construction after *either* is the same as the construction after *or*.

> Jane either cleans the blackboards or she writes an essay.

This sentence is incorrect. In the first clause, *either* follows the subject *Jane*; in the second clause, *or* is before the subject *she*. The sentence can be corrected to read the following ways:

> Either Jane cleans the blackboards or she writes an essay.
>
> Jane either cleans the blackboards or writes an essay.

Exercise 68

Directions: Underline the parallel items and put parentheses around the correlatives.

Example: John plays *(neither)* <u>tennis</u> *(nor)* <u>golf</u>.

1. Bob is not only a fine musician but also an excellent basketball player.

2. Either Jerry finishes his assignment or he will fail the course.

3. Either I will borrow the book from the library or I will buy it.

4. The gymnasium will be used not only for athletic events but also for dances.

5. Whether he stays in school or goes to work must be his decision.

6. I approve of neither your attitude nor your actions.

7. She will probably ask either Caroline or Michelle to go with her.

8. Jack is not only an excellent student but also a fine young man.

9. Either he is justified by his remarks or he is proved guilty.

10. Both the principal and his secretary will attend the meeting.

11. The old man owned neither a coat nor a hat.

12. The teacher asked whether Jane or I had taken her book from her desk.

13. Both blue and yellow drapes were brought to her room.

14. The accident was blamed not only on Bob but also on the entire club.

15. Either he forged the check or he destroyed it.

Exercise 69

Directions: Rewrite each sentence so that all ideas it are expressed consistently.

Example: She either comes late or she forgets her book. *Either she comes late or she forgets her book.*

1. I enjoy working at the store, skiing at Mammoth, and to practice ice skating at our rink.

2. Albert had signed up either for AP calculus or physics.

3. I neither have the time nor the patience for his continually rude conduct.

4. Joe wants either to be a doctor or a veterinarian.

5. He neither had eaten nor slept for two days.

6. This problem should not only be considered by the president of the firm but also by the vice president.

7. Not only is she a fantastic swimmer but she is a fabulous dancer as well.

8. You must not only know how to take pictures but also how to develop them.

9. Everyone admires her courage, but her actions are admired by no one.

10. I could neither go to the right nor to the left.

11. She is neither very brilliant or very stupid.

12. You can either go to the baseball convention or to the basketball convention.

13. You really either ought to telephone your mother or stop to see her.

14. You can either get your tickets in the office or in the gym.

15. I neither was upset nor angry with George.

Semicolons in Series

Semicolons, as you have already studied, can join independent clauses.

> John earned his letterman sweater last year; Bob hopes to earn his this season.

Semicolons also are used to separate items in which there are other commas.

> Jerry was the captain of the team; Paul, the cocaptain; and Pete, the manager.

> Mary joined the Booster Club; John, the Chess Club; and Jill, the Educational Opportunity Club.

Exercise 70

Directions: Punctuate the following sentences correctly. Do not break the sentences.

Example: Try a piece of pie it is your favorite. *Try a piece of pie; it is your favorite.*

1. Last night there was a heavy fog the airport was closed until morning.

2. The population of New Mexico grows each year everyone loves the climate.

3. Jerry was elected the president of the senior class Cindy the vice-president Lori the secretary and Brian the treasurer.

4. If you enjoy traveling, visit Hong Kong this summer it will be an unforgettable trip.

5. We all knew that Bill was not well enough to play however he was determined to try.

6. Matt Fowler who is the school's top football player enjoys soccer as well he plans to play football next year at the Air Force Academy.

7. Because Martha is interested in medicine she plans to major in this field after college she wants to spend her life helping the sick.

8. Jim wants to be an artist Bob an engineer and Raymond an elementary school teacher.

9. That the diplomatic service needs a complete revision was Senator Norman's statement he stressed the need of a committee to study the problem.

10. Try me you'll soon find out what I can do.

11. My car which was in the accident last night is totaled I hope my insurance will help me buy a new one.

12. Try on this sweater it is your favorite color.

13. His argument has some merit however it goes too far.

14. Among those present were Dr. J. Jones president of MWC Albert C. Pyle superintendent of schools B. Crawley manager of the Hilton Hotel and E. T. Miller secretary of the Brown Corporation.

15. Although I seldom have trouble with grammar I have much trouble with punctuation the rules never seem to be consistent.

16. Carrying more than his share of the load Bob hurt his back.

17. It was an exercise in patience but it also became an exercise in endurance.

18. Life according to the philosopher is a battle of wits.

19. Seeing her standing by the candy counter Sam slipped out the back door.

20. I couldn't solve the problem nor could I find anyone else to help me.

Directions: In the following paragraph written by a student, punctuate each sentence correctly.

In *Lord of the Flies* by William Golding external action reveals the personalities of the main characters. Through their actions and external conflicts Ralph becomes the voice of reason Jack the savagery of man and Simon the embodiment of truth. From the beginning of the story Ralph represents the guidance of civilized reason. Concerned with the common good and with justice he strives to establish a sense of law and order on the island. Since his main concern is to be rescued he insists on the signal fire and chides Jack for letting it go out and ruining their chances of getting rescued. This fire becomes a source of conflict yet Ralph sticks to reason in insisting that it be kept burning. Eventually losing the support of the other boys Ralph ends up an outcast. While he can see the value of retaining the externals of civilization the others don't share his adult view and succumb to savagery. Ralph consequently becomes the last voice of common sense and values on the island. He never totally abandons society in the end he weeps for the end of innocence and the darkness in men's hearts.

Sentence Function

Sentences may be classified according to their purpose: *declarative, imperative, interrogative,* and *exclamatory.*

1. *Declarative sentence*

A **declarative sentence** states a fact or an idea and ends with a period. This type of sentence is used most frequently in speaking and writing.

It will probably rain tomorrow.

The meeting will start at three.

2. *Interrogative sentence*

An **interrogative sentence** asks a question and ends with a question mark.

What is going to happen at school tomorrow?

Where did you put my book?

3. *Imperative sentence*

An **imperative sentence** gives a command, a direction, or makes a request. It generally ends with a period, but it can have an exclamation mark.

You will wash the dishes after dinner.

You should turn left here.

Many imperative sentences do not contain stated subjects, because the subject is understood. Requests are often phrased like questions but do not have a question mark at the end.

Help me carry these bags.

Will you put the package on the table.

4. *Exclamatory sentence*

An **exclamatory sentence** conveys strong emotions and ends with an exclamation mark. An exclamatory sentence can be declarative, interrogative, or imperative.

> Watch what you're doing!

> Where in the world did you put my sweater!

Avoid the overuse of exclamation points.

Exercise 72

Directions: Write *D* for declarative, *IN* for interrogative, *IM* for imperative, or *E* for exclamatory. Then put the correct punctuation at the end of each sentence.

Example: *E*   Look out*!*

_____1.   With whom were you speaking in the hall

_____2.   Cut out those pictures for your art project

_____3.   You should learn to concentrate

_____4.   Watch out for snakes

_____5.   Call for help when you need it

_____6.   I received a new car for my birthday

_____7.   Will you please turn off the lights

_____8.   Wash the windows

_____9.   Where did you go yesterday

_____10. Fire Call the fire department

_____11. The auction next year will be held in November

_____12. Don't shout

_____13. I sent them a letter of condolence

_____14. Did you clean your room

_____15. I saw you leave the gym

_____16. Stop immediately

_____17. How do you know when the cookies are done

_____18. Your essay is poorly written

_____19. Did you buy tickets for the concert

_____20. Will you please take these books to the library

The four basic sentence structures are *simple, complex, compound,* and *compound complex.*

1. *Simple sentence*

A **simple sentence** has only one principal clause; it can have phrases but only one basic pattern.

> John ordered pizza last evening for all his teammates.

There is one basic pattern in the sentence: *John ordered pizza.*

The one basic pattern can have compound subjects, compound predicates, or both.

> Mary and Cindy volunteered to serve in the Ventura soup kitchen each Saturday for a month. (compound subject)

> George studied drama for two years and played the lead role in the school play. (compound predicate)

> Susan and her mother went to Santa Barbara and visited the college there. (compound subject and compound predicate)

2. *Complex sentence*

A **complex sentence** has one independent (principal) clause, and one or more dependent clauses. A complex sentence must have more than one basic pattern, one of which is independent; the other, dependent. There are three dependent clauses: adverb, adjective, and noun.

> Whoever wants this job can have it!

The dependent noun clause *whoever wants this job* is the subject of the independent clause *can have it.*

> After you read the novel, and after you write your book report, we will watch it on video.

The subordinate conjunction *after* is introducing two adverb clauses. The principal clause is *we will watch it.*

> The little old lady who wandered helpless and bewildered down Pico Boulevard was finally rescued.

> The relative clause *who wandered* modifies *lady* in the main clause.

Independent Clause	Dependent Clause
Ralph washed and polished his car	before he went to the dance.
Ralph washed and polished his car	that he received on his birthday.
Please give this book to	whoever asks for it.
Please give this book to	whomever you choose.
Ray gave warm greetings	when he arrived at church.
Ray gave warm greetings	to whomever he saw.

3. *Compound sentence*

A **compound sentence** may have a number of independent clauses, but no dependent clause. The independent clauses are joined either with a comma plus a coordinate conjunction, or with a semicolon when there is no coordinate conjunction.

> Jeff left late last night, but we left early in the morning.

> It is too late to enter the contest; you may, however, volunteer to be a judge.

Conjunctive adverbs do not join clauses. They are used transitionally.

> I did not hear the alarm this morning; consequently, I was late for work.

Independent Clause	Coordinating Conjunction or Semicolon	Independent Clause
They won the game	, but	we had the victory.
John wrote the best essay	;	now the reward is his.
She has been tardy five times	; consequently,	she can't go to the prom.
Jean stays up late at night	; therefore,	she sleeps in class.

4. *Compound-complex sentence*

A **compound-complex sentence** has two or more independent clauses and one or more dependent clauses.

> Although Jerry wanted to go to Tulane, his grades were too poor, and he had to attend junior college for two years.

> Our car ran out of gas, and we had to walk five miles to a gas station; consequently, we missed the basketball game because we were two hours late.

Independent Clauses	Coordinating Construction	Dependent Clause	Kind of Dependent Clause
His grades were poor	, and	although he wanted	adverb
to go to Tulane he had to attend junior college.			
Our car ran out of gas	, and		adverb
we had to walk five miles	; consequently	because we were late	adverb
we missed the basketball game.			

Directions: On a separate piece of paper, write out the basic patterns for dependent and independent clauses, the subordinate conjunction for adverb clauses, the relative pronoun for relative clauses, or the use for the noun clauses.

Example: Who do you think rang the bell?

Independent Clause	Dependent Clause	Subordinate Conjunction, Relative Pronoun, or Use of Noun Clause
you do think	*who rang bell*	*direct object*

1. Although I love football, I never play it.
2. Because Mary forgot to send in her registration, she was disqualified.
3. The news that he was elected president startled everyone.
4. When it started to rain, we left.
5. The flower that I grew for the contest died.
6. The truth is that Tom received a scholarship to the University of Arizona.
7. We all saw the accident that happened on Fourth Street.
8. Do you know what he said?
9. That I wanted to live with my father bothered my mother.
10. We read the news that was in the paper.

Directions: On a separate piece of paper, write ten complex sentences using the suggestions below.

1. Noun clause
2. Relative clause
3. Adverb clause
4. Noun clause as subject
5. Noun clause as direct object
6. Noun clause as subject complement
7. Noun clause as apposition
8. Adverb clause, periodic
9. Relative clause, restrictive
10. Relative clause, nonrestrictive

Directions: Identify the conjunctions in the following sentences as *COR*, correlative; *CO*, coordinate; *S*, subordinate; or *CA*, conjunctive adverb.

Example: _COR_ Both my mother and my sister have brown hair.

_____1. Jane likes tennis, *since* she is an excellent player.

_____2. *Neither* Ellen *nor* Bob has been to a professional football game.

_____3. She has permission to stay until her aunt comes.

_____4. The alarm sounded, *but* my mother never heard it.

_____5. *Either* you get the permission *or* I will.

_____6. I failed the last two exams; *consequently*, I am grounded for the next two weeks.

_____7. The path was hard to find, *for* no one has used it for years.

_____8. We have been fishing for hours, *yet* we haven't caught a single fish.

_____9. Joe is usually on time for school, *but* this morning he was late.

_____10. *When* I am hungry, I eat *both* cereal *and* pancakes for breakfast.

Exercise 76

Directions: Write *S*, simple; *CX*, complex; *CD*, compound; or *CC*, compound-complex for each sentence.

Example: <u>*CD*</u> I have many questions; for instance, how much does the term paper count for our final grade?

_____1. Joe was lost; he had never seen these streets before.

_____2. The trip to Disneyland was fascinating.

_____3. The stone arches that support the steel cables were carefully constructed.

_____4. Because men had to dig deep into the earth, compressed air had to be pumped into the airlocks.

_____5. Are you going to the movies, or are you staying home?

_____6. Gene looked for the book that he had lost, but he could not find it.

_____7. Tim and Larry, my friends for many years, will be visiting me next week.

_____8. You can study in my room, or if you prefer, you can study in the library.

_____9. Michelle returned her library books yesterday.

_____10. You can do the dishes, or you can vacuum your room.

_____11. Mr. Jones, an able reporter, covered the trial for the local newspaper; however, few of the spectators were satisfied with his articles.

_____12. The cat usually sits near Richard's room, but when anyone comes around, she races down the hall.

_____13. The teacher's job was to instruct the handicapped.

_____14. Our basketball team is raising money for some new uniforms, and next week they will be holding a candy sale that should raise $5,000.

_____15. Richard is a better fisherman than I.

_____16. Once it erupted, Krakatoa spewed smoke and clouds of black ash up to seven miles high.

_____17. The sound, which has been called the loudest ever, was heard for thousands of miles, and the shock waves were felt halfway around the world.

_____18. At first, no one knew what had happened.

_____19. Ash-laden skies caused unusually vivid sunset for years until the particles finally settled.

_____20. Life has returned, but no one knows when Krakatoa will erupt again.

Exercise 77

Directions: Identify each sentence's function as *D*, declarative; *IN*, interrogative; *IM*, imperative; or *E*, exclamatory. Add punctuation marks.

Example: *IM*   Put the clean laundry away.

_____1.   Let the dough rise in a warm place for about an hour

_____2.   Where did you put the beach towels

_____3.   What a rude thing to say

_____4.   My friend sent me a letter

_____5.   Please send me your address

_____6.   Never do that again

_____7.   Have you visited your cousin this week

_____8.   Our new car is red

_____9.   Glue the two pieces together

_____10. Watch out

Exercise 78

Directions: Identify each sentence's structure as *S*, simple; *CD*, compound; *CX*, complex; or *CC*, compound-complex.

Example: *S*   I often get hungry before dinnertime.

_____1.   If you like math, be sure to take Calculus II.

_____2.   Noticing his dilemma, I took him by the arm and led him out of the room.

_____3.   The job that was offered me seemed hard and complicated; nevertheless, I decided to give it a try.

_____4.   The principal smiled graciously and shook hands with each guest.

_____5.   The project seemed impossible to complete; nevertheless, we managed to finish it in two weeks.

_____6.   Paul looked down at the pool, looked around to see if anyone was watching, took a deep breath, and jumped.

_____7.   Jack finished his homework early, and then he decided to meet his friends at the drug store.

_____8.   We stood outside the hotel waiting for the rain to stop.

_____9.   I thought the boy looked familiar, but I soon discovered that he was a perfect stranger.

_____10. Bob picked up the ball and threw it at the fence.

Unit 6

Mood, Potential, Parallelism, Transitions

Mood of Verbs

The word *mood* in grammatical construction is the speakers' attitude toward what is being expressed, whether it is a fact or contrary to fact, a wish or a command. There are three moods of verbs: *indicative*, *imperative*, and *subjunctive*.

1. *Indicative mood*

The **indicative mood** is used to make a statement or ask a question. Almost all of the verbs you use in speaking or writing are in the indicative mood.

> Are you going to the game?

> My brother wants to go to Colorado this summer.

2. *Imperative mood*

The **imperative mood** is used to express commands or requests. Even when *please* is added, the verb is still imperative.

> Please take this book to the library.

> Sit up straight.

The indicative and the imperative moods do not change the forms of the verb, but the subjunctive mood does change the verb form.

3. *Subjunctive mood*

The **subjunctive mood** does not state a fact, but represents an act or state of being as a contingency or possibility.

Conjugation of the Subjunctive Mood

The present tense of the irregular verb is always *be*.

I be	we be
you be	you be
he, she, it be	they be

The past tense of the irregular verb is always *were*.

I were	we were
you were	you were
he, she, it were	they were

In regular verbs the *s* is omitted in the third person, singular.

he have	she write	it begin

Uses of the Subjunctive Mood

The subjunctive mood, although often replaced by the indicative mood in writing and speaking, has two important uses in contemporary English:

a. *It expresses a demand, recommendation, suggestion, wish, hope or necessity.*

> The teacher demanded that Joe report to the principal's office immediately.

The mood of the verb is subjunctive. If Joe actually performs the act, the sentence would be *Joe reports to the principal's office.*

> I suggest that she take Spanish next semester.

The sentence does not state that she takes Spanish. It is only a suggestion.

> It is necessary that Tom be home by dark.

This is a statement of necessity.

> God bless you.

This does not mean that God is blessing you. It is a hope or desire that God will bless you.

> "If this be treason!" said Patrick Henry.

He is careful to say *"if this be."* He is not stating that it is treason.

b. *It states a condition or wish that is contrary to fact.*

> If Sarah were the principal, things might be a lot better.

Sarah is not the principal: the condition is contrary to fact.

> I wish I were a genius.

This is a wish that is contrary to fact.

Exercise 79

Directions: Underline the errors in the following sentences and rewrite each sentence correctly.

Example: Jack walks as if he <u>was</u> lame. *Jack walks as if he were lame.*

1. I wish my brother was with me during this time.

2. I only hope that he keeps his appointment; otherwise, I will miss the entire performance.

3. It is necessary that the photographer gets you to look at the camera.

4. She complained to me as if I was in charge.

5. It is suggested that the photographer keeps the background uncluttered.

6. If I was the President, I would have no more homeless people or hunger.

7. It is necessary in her job that she remains healthy.

8. I wish I was a champion tennis player.

9. I recommend that you are careful when driving.

10. If this is reality, I would rather be dreaming.

11. I suggest that you are paying attention.

12. He looks as if he was going to faint.

13. If Joe was a little older, he might have more sense.

14. If only he was twenty.

15. If this was war, I would enlist immediately.

16. If Tom was more sociable, he would have many more friends.

17. The teacher suggested that Jane takes another course in math.

18. I suggest that Bob was less formal.

19. If Jane was elected tomorrow, we would all celebrate.

20. I wish that Joe was more tactful and considerate.

Exercise 80

Directions: On a separate piece of paper, write original sentences using the suggestions for each sentence.

1. Contrary to fact
2. Necessity
3. Hope
4. Suggestion

5. Demand
6. Desire
7. Wish
8. Contrary to fact

Review

The indicative mood makes a statement or asks a question. The imperative mood expresses commands or requests. The subjunctive mood represents an act or state of being as a contingency or possibility.

Potential Form of Verbs

Potential means *existing in possibility*. This is exactly what the potential form of the verb means. Once that act is performed, it is no longer potential.

The potential forms of the verb are as follows:

Present tense	Past tense
may	might
can	could
must	should
	would

The auxiliary verb *have* is also used with these verbs.

1. *may, might*

The verb means "permission to do something."

> May I leave the room?

> John says that he might go fishing tomorrow morning.

In each of the sentences, the verb shows that the activity in question is permitted to occur.

2. *can, could*

The verb means "the ability to do something."

> I can lift that box.

> She could beat him at tennis.

In each of the sentences, the verb shows that the activity in question is capable of being done.

3. *must, should*

The verb means "obligation to do something."

> I must visit my aunt in the hospital.

> She should mail the letter immediately.

In each of the sentences, the verb shows that the activity in question needs to be done.

4. *would*

The verb means "desire or intent to do something."

I would certainly do that if I could.

He would have taken the book to the library, but he had no time.

In each sentence, the verb shows that the subject wishes or plans to do the activity in question.

Correct Usage with Potential Verbs

1. Do not use the potential verb with the conditional.

If I would have seen you, I would have greeted you. (Incorrect)

If I had seen you, I would have greeted you. (Correct)

2. If you are writing an essay in the present tense, use *can, may,* or *must.*

3. If you are writing an essay in the past tense, use *could, should, would,* or *might.*

The most important part of this study is the correct usage explained above. Be especially careful not to use the potential form with a conditional clause.

Exercise 81

Directions: Underline the errors and correctly rewrite the sentence.

Example: If he <u>would</u> <u>have</u> <u>read</u> the book, he would have known the answer. *If he had read the book, he would have known the answer.*

1. If you would have sent us your resume, we might have hired you.

2. John said that he may go with us to the game on Friday night.

3. If you would have been willing to practice more frequently, you would have been a better skater.

4. Jerry agreed that we may finish our project in time to enter it into the science fair.

5. Mother said that I can go to the show.

6. If you would have attended the meeting, you would have known the major problem.

7. Jeannie's mother said that Jeannie can attend the concert on Friday night.

8. The old lady says that I might help her to weed her lawn on Saturday morning.

9. Margie said that I must take a course in art if I plan to go to college in the fall.

10. The coach said that I can beat Jeff in tennis if I practiced harder.

Parallel Structure

Parallelism is writing consistently by using the same grammatical construction. Words, phrases, or clauses that are parallel in function should also be parallel in grammatical form.

> Tom is good at writing essays, illustrating stories, and tennis. (Incorrect)
>
> Tom is good at writing essays, illustrating stories, and playing tennis. (Correct)

1. *Parallel words*

> The school's philosophy included all aspects of a student's life: intellectual, social, physical, and moral.

2. *Parallel phrases*

> You must always find time for doing your homework, for getting enough rest, and for exercising.
>
> Tom enjoys working with rockets, animals, and computers. (The preposition can be understood.)

3. *Parallel clauses*

> We all knew why Bill had earned the trip to Russia, what he planned to do when he arrived there, and how long he planned to stay.
>
> The teacher gives extra time to students who are industrious, who are trustworthy, and who are capable of profiting from the extra attention.

Ways to Avoid Faulty Parallelism

1. Express ideas of equal importance in equal grammatical constructions.

> Last year I took piano lessons, joined the volleyball team, and volunteered at the hospital.

> We bake cakes on Tuesdays, wash clothes on Wednesdays, and get groceries on Thursdays.

Exercise 82

Directions: Rewrite the following sentences, making them parallel.

1. The entire team ordered hamburgers with cheese and onions, ice cream, and for a drink they had Diet Pepsi.

2. On our end-of-the-year picnic, our class enjoyed barbecuing hamburgers, hiking through the woods, and to play baseball in the park.

3. The teacher asked us whether we preferred going to Magic Mountain, that we could go swimming at Lake Sherman, or enjoy a Dodger baseball game.

2. Use correlatives to connect sentence elements that are in parallel form.

> We need to not only study harder, but also to take better notes.

> Jeff can play neither the piano nor the guitar.

Exercise 83

Directions: Rewrite the following sentences, correcting the use of correlatives.

1. Jean not only is editor of the school paper but also of our yearbook.

2. Paul either is on top of the world, or he is deep in the abyss.

3. Mary is neither a good student or a good worker.

4. He neither plays football nor basketball.

5. Not only is Paul planning to be a physician he is also planning to specialize in pediatrics.

3. Avoid shifting voice and person.

> As we entered the room, you could hear a pin drop. (Incorrect, shift in person)
>
> As we entered the room, we could hear a pin drop. (Correct)
>
> I wrote a poem for the yearbook, but it was rejected by the editor. (Incorrect, shift in voice)
>
> I wrote a poem for the yearbook, but the editor rejected it. (Correct)

Exercise 84

Directions: Rewrite the following sentences, correcting the errors.

1. The girls in the class prepared a delicious lunch, but it was gobbled down by the boys.

2. When you go to your first prom, everyone wants to look his/her very best.

3. The freshmen decorated the gym for the welcome dance, but their decorations were criticized by the seniors.

4. My sister and I tried out for the school play, and I was chosen for the lead.

5. Joe turned in the best composition, but it was laughed at by his friends.

4. Comparisons must always be complete and reasonable.

Our track team is as fast, if not faster, than yours.

We can't say *our track team is as fast than yours*. The expression *if not faster* should follow the complete comparison.

> Our track team is as fast as yours, if not faster.
>
> Our track team is as fast as, if not faster than, yours.
>
> I can write better than Jane.

Here the comparison is not clear.

> I can write better than Jane writes.

Exercise 85

Directions: Rewrite the above sentences, correcting the errors.

1. I can throw the ball farther than Pete.

2. Her hair is just like her mother.

3. Jane is as happy if not happier than Michelle, her friend.

4. His voice is as good if not better than Brian.

5. Jeff's ability to write was like his brother.

Exercise 86

Directions: Correct the errors in parallel structure in the following sentences.

Example: You will be accepted by a good college if you join school clubs, earn good grades, and by scoring over 1400 on the SAT. *You will be accepted by a good college if you join school clubs, earn good grades, and score over 1400 on the SAT.*

1. My brother prefers staying home to parties.

2. He was pleased less by the recognition of his abilities than what he had accomplished.

3. By studying for the examination and not worried about the results, you will probably be more successful.

4. He was chosen because of his ability rather than he was a good leader.

5. We all decided to go out for pizza rather than going to an expensive restaurant.

6. Remember that working hard in high school is commendable, but that to try to do too much is foolish.

7. Because Tom was an excellent student, because he was determined and conscientious, and that he wanted to be a doctor, he was given an academic scholarship to Duke University.

8. The class decided to visit the museum and seeing everything on display.

9. His efforts are as great if not greater than Ted.

10. Mabel either will go to Georgia Tech and study engineering or go to Occidental and study music.

11. They discussed firing the manager, hiring a replacement, and to change the pitching staff.

12. At the picnic we played ball in the park while all the lunch was eaten by the spectators.

13. This situation should not only be considered by the coach but also by the players.

14. Jerry built model airplanes in order to fly them and because he enjoyed building them.

15. When the bell rang for class, the doors were opened by the principal.

16. Jack not only belongs to the soccer team, but also the golf team.

17. I play the piano as well if not better than Jean.

18. I enjoy playing the organ, singing in the choir, and to help organize concerts.

19. We all gathered in the auditorium to listen to his talk but little attention was paid by several of the students.

20. Giving a speech before a large audience can require more courage than to take the SAT.

Exercise 87

Directions: On a separate piece of paper, write original sentences with parallel structure using the suggestions given below.

1. Use *and* to join two or more parallel prepositional phrases.
2. Use *and* to join two or more parallel gerund phrases.
3. Use *and* to join parallel infinitive phrases.
4. Use *and* to join parallel subordinate clauses.
5. Use *and* to join parallel independent clauses.
6. Write a sentence using a correlative.
7. Write a sentence beginning with "Playing baseball is much more exciting than."
8. Write a sentence using parallel words.
9. Write a sentence using parallel phrases.
10. Write a sentence using parallel clauses.

Exercise 88

Directions: On a separate piece of paper, revise the following paragraph. You can combine sentences to create a variety of sentence lengths, structures, and beginnings. Correct any grammatical errors or faulty parallelism.

> A football player has a great job. It is not an easy job. He has to spend many hours each day practicing. He has to listen to the coach and the manager. The coach often yells at him. He has to take criticism and sarcasm. He often has to suffer many types of injuries. Often while playing, a whole team will tackle him, not just once but many times during a game. He has to enjoy playing the game more than the injuries he receives. A football player must be dedicated to the game. He studies and memorizes many plays. Various strategies are practiced over and over again. Each strategy is gone over many times until they are perfect. The game is always videotaped. The various plays are studied during a film session. Mistakes are pointed out as well as good plays. This is done so that mistakes will not be repeated. A good player is always trying to be better. He enjoys being part of the game. He enjoys the cheers of the fans. He enjoys the excitement. Best of all he enjoys winning and being part of the team.

Exercise 89

Directions: On a separate piece of paper, revise the following paragraph by organizing the material so that ideas follow logically. Eliminate anything that is not pertinent or that is repetitious.

> One of the themes explored by Emily Brontë in *Wuthering Heights* is parent/child relationships. She suggests that children are naturally rebellious. Adults cannot restrain them. Hindley was a father figure to Cathy. He forbade her to see Heathcliff. He never liked Heathcliff. This edict brought the two together more than ever. One time she climbed through a skylight in the garret to be with him. She did this after Hindley had banished Heathcliff from the house. The more Hindley tried to separate the two, the more they were together. Isabella, too, was determined not to be restrained. She fell in love with Heathcliff. Edgar, who was her brother, was in charge of her after the death of the Lintons. He told Isabella that she was never to see Heathcliff, and he told Heathcliff never to return to the Grange. Shortly after this incident, Isabella eloped with Heathcliff. She soon regretted her behavior. Brontë seems to make a strong point: the more rules, the more restraints, the greater the rebellion. She is not suggesting that rebellion from authority is good. It is just inevitable.

Exercise 90

Directions: Revise the following sentences.

Example: He wore a blue jacket, a shirt with blue and white stripes, tan pants, and tan shoes. *He wore a blue jacket, a blue and white striped shirt, tan pants, and tan shoes.*

1. Bob likes to swim, play cards, and go dancing.

2. Liz was as happy if not happier over the outcome of the debate than Peggy.

3. Lois was lively, athletic, and everybody liked her.

4. The principal neither informed the faculty nor the parents about the outcome of the questionnaire.

5. Playing baseball, Jerry broke the window and it was replaced immediately.

6. The baseball team either could choose to go to a baseball game or going to an amusement park.

7. We bought a board six feet long and two feet in width.

8. Kevin's walk was like a bear.

9. The weather in Chicago is as cold if not colder than New York.

10. John pitched the first six innings and the final three were pitched by Dave.

Variety in Sentence Structure

Changing a sentence into a dependent clause or phrase and inserting it into another sentence is a good combining technique and a way to reduce wordiness in writing. There is generally more than one way to combine sentences.

> Base: Mary is excellent in math.

> Insert: She plans to major in engineering at Purdue next year.

These two sentences can be changed and combined to make the following sentences.

> Mary, who is excellent in math, plans to major in engineering at Purdue next year.

The base sentence was changed to a relative clause.

> An excellent math student, Mary plans to major in engineering at Purdue next year.

The base sentence was changed to apposition.

> Base: The senior class was permitted to go to Magic Mountain.

> Insert: It was an outstanding class of scholars and athletes.

> Because it was an outstanding class of scholars and athletes, the senior class was permitted to go to Magic Mountain.

The insert sentence was changed to an adverb clause.

> Base: Jim played both football and baseball.

> Insert: Jim lettered in two varsity sports.

> Playing both football and baseball, Jim lettered in two varsity sports.

The base sentence was changed to a participial phrase.

Exercise 91

Directions: The base sentence is given. On a separate piece of paper, make up another sentence; then combine the two. State what change you made.

Example: Base: The fight on the school grounds was both violent and vicious.

> *Insert: The principal knew about the fight.*

> *Combination: The principal knew that the fight on the school grounds was violent and vicious.*

> *Change: Base sentence changed to a noun clause.*

1. Jerry won the VIP trophy.
2. My father discovered a so-called cure for baldness.
3. Alice took first place in the city's track meet.
4. My father bought an old farmhouse outside of town.
5. Angela received help to meet many of her expenses at college.
6. Laurel and Hardy successfully moved from silent motion pictures to movies with sound.
7. Colleen entered the Chicago Beauty Pageant for teenagers.
8. Ken was seriously injured in the accident.
9. Arthur was an outstanding baseball player.
10. Joe will be giving an all-day concert in Lexington.

Other Ways to Add Variety to Sentences

1. Use different constructions at the beginning of sentences.

> Learning to work with computers is essential today. (gerund)
>
> To work at such a fast pace can bring about stress. (infinitive)
>
> On the sidewalk, boys were arguing. (prepositional phrase)
>
> Swiftly, Ted ran around the track. (adverb)
>
> Discouraged and frustrated, I left the room in tears. (participles)
>
> After you choose your partner, you may leave. (adverb clause—periodic)
>
> Bored and unhappy, I joined the meeting. (adjectives)
>
> The tide coming in, we headed for shore. (nominative absolute)
>
> That he was unable to understand the problem was clearly evident. (noun clause)

2. Occasionally insert a question, an exclamation, or a command.

> What should we do?
>
> Where do you think this is taking us?
>
> Watch out for rocks!
>
> Leave and never return.
>
> "Did you break my test tubes?" I shouted.

3. Occasionally use appropriate words between the subject and the predicate.

> The tunnel, dark and damp, made him ill.
>
> Bill, frustrated and discouraged, left the meeting.
>
> Jill, who enjoys skiing, plans to go to Mammoth next week.

Exercise 92

Directions: Vary the word order in the following sentences without destroying the original meaning. Shorten sentences when possible.

Example: I was late for soccer practice because I had a detention. *Since I had a detention, I was late for soccer practice.*

1. Pete decided to finish the job in the morning if no one interrupted him.

2. It was a fact that Jeff wanted to be elected president of the company his father owned.

3. She received the news of his death when she was listening to the radio early in the morning.

4. Patricia is the brightest girl in the senior class, and she was chosen to be the class representative at the Youths' Congress.

5. We went to the refreshment stand during the game, and there we bought hamburgers and Cokes.

6. She asked me what I did with her book. (use direct quotes)

7. She likes to interfere with the chess players by asking them questions during their game.

8. You will not be chosen for the team unless you come to practice every day.

9. However, it is certainly true that no one knew what they were doing.

10. Jenny plans to be a doctor someday, and she enjoys doing volunteer work at the hospital.

Clear Transitions and Reference

Connectives give the exact relation between ideas.

>   We all went to the game *although* it was still raining.
>   We all went to the game *while* it was still raining.
>   We all went to the game *because* it was still raining.

What is the difference in meaning made by the italicized connectives?

The following connectives are often used incorrectly.

When, than

When means "at that time."

>   It began to rain when we went out to play.

Than suggests a comparison.

>   She is a better player than Tim.

How, that, because

With noun clauses, use *that*; never a subordinate conjunction.

> We all saw how he was growing old.

This is incorrect because we're not concerned with how he was growing old. The following sentence is correct.

> We all saw that he was growing old.

Is is a linking verb and should never be followed by a subordinate conjunction, as it is in the following incorrect sentence.

> The reason he could not go is *because* he was ill.

Is must be followed by a noun, pronoun, or adjective, as in the following correct sentence.

> The truth is that John is too lazy to write letters.

Although, while

Although means "in spite of the fact."

> He always played well although he never made the team.

While means "during that time."

> He enjoyed a well-deserved vacation while I was working.

If, whether

If is a subordinate conjunction expressing condition and should be used with conditional clauses.

> *If* you plan to leave early, I will go with someone else.

Whether expresses doubt or two possible choices and should be used with noun clauses.

> I doubt whether he will win the race.

Position of Modifiers

The placement of words within a sentence is very important.

> Faculty members are required to attend *only* one workshop.

> *Only* faculty members are required to attend one workshop.

The first sentence means that the requirement is for one workshop; the second means that the requirement applies to faculty members and no one else.

1. *Modifier placement*

Usually put a single-word modifier close to the word it modifies.

> Only Sue planned to host the next meeting.

> Sue only planned to host the next meeting.

> Sue planned to host only the next meeting.

Possible meanings:

Sue was the one who was going to host the next meeting.

Sue planned to host the next meeting, but nothing else.

Sue would host the next meeting, but no other meetings.

2. *Modifying phrases*

Place modifying phrase close to the part of the sentence it modifies.

> The piano was sold to Tom with wooden legs.

This is incorrect, unless Tom does happen to have wooden legs. The correct sentence would be *The piano with the wooden legs was sold to Tom.*

Relative clauses should be as close as possible to the nouns they modify.

> My friend went to Australia who is a tennis fan.
>
> *My friend who is a tennis fan went to Australia.*

3. *Squinting modifiers*

A squinting modifier can modify either the words before it or the words after it.

> Terry promised when the basketball game was over that she would leave.

The adverb clause is squinting here because it is modifying the main clause as well as the noun clause.

> Terry promised that she would leave when the basketball game was over.

4. *Dangling modifier*

A modifier that does not logically modify any word or words in the same sentence is called dangling.

> Writing the letter quickly in order to mail it on time, the fountain pen leaked.

Revising the sentence will make its meaning clearer.

> I was trying to finish the letter and mail it on time, but my pen leaked.
>
> To succeed in school, much studying is required.
>
> *Students must study in order to succeed in school.*

5. *Dangling clauses*

Clauses also can be dangling if the subject of the main clause is not the same subject as in the dependent clause.

> While practicing tackling during football practice, the coach made us all do laps.

The coach is not practicing tackling, so this sentence needs to be revised.

> While we were practicing tackling during football practice, we had to do laps.

Exercise 93

Directions: Revise the following sentences.

Example: When only five years old, the teacher realized that Jane could read as well as her fifth-grade students. *When Jane was only five years old, she could read as well as fifth-grade students.*

1. I only read one novel this summer.

2. To complete my term paper, some research is still needed.

3. While studying computer literacy, new methods for writing papers were learned.

4. John agreed that when the dance was over he would go straight home.

5. When I saw the sunset, a feeling of awe came over me.

6. Racing hurriedly to get to school on time, my shoelaces broke.

7. While standing in the ball park, an airplane flew overhead.

8. Many people asked if we had extra tickets to the concert.

9. The real reason why he is not playing in the game tonight is because he was suspended for being truant last Friday.

10. We drove to the concert where Jim was scheduled to sing in my car.

Eliminating Deadwood

Unnecessary words or phrases that take up space without furthering the meaning of a sentence are **deadwood**.

Kinds of Deadwood

1. *Empty words*

   These words add length but contribute nothing to the ideas presented.

in my opinion	you know
it is true that	needless to say
it is often agreed	Mr. Jones, he
despite the fact	what I mean is
I think	I am firmly convinced
the type of	again and again

2. *Hedging*

   This occurs when a statement is made and then these words are used to back away from that statement or water down the idea.

almost	possibly
somewhat	sort of
could be	well, I'm not sure
it seems	not exactly
very much aware	

Exercise 94

Directions: Rewrite the following sentences, eliminating all deadwood.

Example: There are several reasons my father gave us for the reason why he thought we should not go to the meeting. *My father gave several reasons why we should not go to the meeting.*

1. The reason he gave was that he thought we were not ready to handle the project without supervision.

2. It seems that the principal thought that the freshmen were too immature to sponsor a dance.

3. I am somewhat bewildered by the turn of events that took place this evening.

4. I think that football should be eliminated from college campuses because it has been proved not beneficial because it often causes physical injury to the body.

5. As I often repeated over and over again that the main point is that the school should not tolerate tardiness.

6. The reason that we did not want to attend the game was because we were afraid that it would interfere with an important exam the next day.

7. The boy who was handing out leaflets before the show really is hoping to become an actor someday.

8. Miss Powers, the math teacher, is always willing to give help to you if you are willing to ask her.

9. When Bob walked into the gym, the girls kind of crowded around him.

10. Jennifer told the class that her brother, who is trying out for the Olympics, has been swimming and diving since he was six years old.

3. _Redundancy_

This is the unnecessary repetition of an idea which results in weakened writing.

Exercise 95

Directions: Revise the following sentences, eliminating anything that is redundant.

Example: He has a big backpack that is blue and has a lot of room for books. _He has a big blue backpack._

1. I endorsed the check on the back.

2. We bought a round trip ticket to and from Chicago.

3. She advanced to the front of the room and read from her paper.

4. The car I bought last week is dark blue in color.

5. Joe is a negligent driver because he is so careless.

6. When he reached his own room by himself, Ted took a book and started to read.

7. I retraced my steps back to where I started from.

8. My sister stood up and spoke aloud to the class.

9. We are going to vote for the incumbent candidate who is now in office.

10. The consensus of everyone's opinion was radically opposed to having an all-year school year.

11. The room is 8 feet in length by 6 feet in width and is 10 feet high.

12. Gerard Manley Hopkins, the author of "God's Grandeur," he gives a clear-cut picture of how man is ruining his environment.

13. It is an asset to have a really fine camera, but actually it is not really necessary.

14. I have always thoroughly enjoyed reading the plays by Shakespeare because he has a lot of excitement and suspense in them.

15. I would like you to go over your assignment carefully so that you are positive you have eliminated every possible error.

Exercise 96

Directions: On a separate piece of paper, revise the following paragraph.

I had just returned from college for a much-needed summer vacation. My friends and I decided to spend a leisurely afternoon at the lake, which is just about three miles from my house. Lake Horne is a very popular resort. We enjoy all types of fun the lake provides: swimming, boating, fishing, and sometimes just to sit and dangle our feet in the water. This particular afternoon we were sitting on the bank talking over our experiences of the past year. Each one had their own story to tell. Suddenly, without warning, four young men invaded our territory; they were yelling. One of the boys was brandishing a gun. We were all stunned for a moment, and could hardly do anything. Just then Bob, who is the elder of our group, picked up a stick that was lying within reach and threw it at the boy with the gun. The stick struck the gun; it went off, but no one was hurt. By that time we were able to capture two of the boys, and the other two boys ran for their lives. When the police arrived, we told them our story and went home. We were saddened at what happened to ruin a quiet afternoon.

Exercise 97

Directions: Revise the following sentences.

Example: To handle that situation delicately, tact must be used. *Tact must be used when handling delicate situations.*

1. The fans were angry and frustrated. They surged on the baseball field and booed the umpire.

2. My little brother with his friends went into the kitchen and the cookie jar was taken from the counter.

3. Kathy and her friends decided to go to San Francisco to visit my cousin recently.

4. We certainly enjoyed the basketball game and the victory was celebrated by both team and fans at McDonald's.

5. She neither is very dependable or loyal, we had to fire her.

6. It was decided by the entire senior class to hold a farewell party after graduation immediately.

7. By the way, we will let you know how much you owe and what you can do about payments.

8. Personally, I think that we should continue the project, but cut down on the countless hours of work we are putting into it.

9. We were asked recently by the principal to give our honest opinion about school uniforms.

10. Hoping to go to UCLA, study and getting high SAT scores became my first priority.

Italics

Italic type, used by the printer, is a slanted type. To indicate italics in typing or writing, we underline. Today, electronic typewriters, computers, and word processors have an italic element.

When to Italicize

As a general rule, use italics when the material can be published separately.

1. A novel is published separately, so titles of novels must be italicized. A short story is not published separately, so quotation marks are used.

> *Lord of the Flies*
>
> "The Haircut"

2. Magazines are published separately, but articles, stories, or poems that are in magazines should have quotation marks.

> *Sports Illustrated*
>
> "Who Will Win the Rose Bowl?"

3. Newspapers are italicized. The article at the beginning of the title (*the, a, an*) is not usually italicized.

> the *Los Angeles Times*

4. Italicize full-length plays; use quotation marks for one-act plays.

> *Macbeth*
>
> "Trifles"

5. Italicize films and TV shows (lengthy or short), works of art, ships, trains, airplanes, spacecrafts, and court cases.

> *Star Wars* (film)
>
> *Saturday Night Live* (TV show)
>
> *Mona Lisa* (painting)
>
> *Clermont* (boat)
>
> *Wabash Cannonball* (train)
>
> *Spirit of St. Louis* (airplane)
>
> *Sputnik* (spacecraft)
>
> *Plessy v. Ferguson* (court case)

6. Italicize words, letters, numerals, and symbols used to represent themselves.

> The *t* is broken on my typewriter.
>
> What does *discriminate* mean?

7. Italicize to indicate that a word is still considered a foreign element.

> *Au contraire,* the work was finished already.
>
> If you go to Hawaii, you'll learn what *mahalo* means.

Exercise 98

Directions: In the following sentences, underline the words that should be italicized and add quotation marks where necessary.

Example: She always stumbles over the word <u>Mississippi</u>.

1. We read the novel Madame Bovary last semester.

2. Mary Shelley wrote the novel Frankenstein.

3. The Brady Bunch is one of several television shows that have been made into movies.

4. Did you read Our Schools Need Help in the Reader's Digest?

5. We watched the TV show Home Improvement last night.

6. My sister frequently mispronounces evening.

7. We studied Richard III in our junior English class last year.

8. The s and t are not clear on my typewriter.

9. The Scholastic Magazine is used in our English classes.

10. We had to read at least two articles from the Los Angeles Times for our history report.

11. Our class visited the museum where we saw a reproduction of the Mona Lisa.

12. There is no e following the g in the word judgment.

13. My father enjoys watching Candid Camera.

14. Possibly one of the most famous airplanes is the Spirit of St. Louis.

15. In the short story Judas, by Frank O'Connor, the narrator reveals his anxiety in trying to escape from his mother's dominance.

16. Have you ever read the poem Cats by T. S. Eliot?

17. Cats was made into a musical called Cats.

18. Robinson Crusoe was the first novel I ever read.

19. Aunt Helen has seen every episode of I Love Lucy ever shown on TV.

20. John's savoir-faire prevented an embarrassing situation.

Troublesome Word Usage

Many of the following words are used incorrectly in writing. Study these words carefully to master their exact meanings.

1. *adapt, adopt*

   Adapt means "to adjust."

   > It was difficult for her to adapt to India's climate.

   Adopt means "to take as one's own."

   > My mother adopted a baby girl.

2. *accept, except*

   Accept means "to receive."

   > She accepted his praise.

   Except is a preposition meaning "to leave out" or "other than."

   > All may go to the game except Pete.

3. *accuse, allege*

   Accuse means "to blame."

   > The teacher accused me of talking during the test.

   Allege means "to claim something that is yet to be proven."

   > The report alleged that the older man committed the crime.

4. *affect, effect*

   Affect is usually a verb meaning "to influence."

   > How did the medicine affect your nervous system?

   Effect can be used both as a noun and a verb. As a noun, it means "result."

   > I hope you know the effect drugs can have on your mind.

   As a verb, *effect* means "to cause."

   > He will effect some changes.

5. *allot, a lot*

   Allot is a verb meaning "to assign as a share or portion."

   > Her father allotted her a weekly allowance of $10.

   A lot means "a great many."

   > We visited a lot of states last summer.

   Note: There is no such word as *alot*.

6. *aggravate, irritate*

   Aggravate means "to make worse."

   > Tension aggravated my headache.

   Irritate means "to provoke, to exasperate."

   > The boy irritated his teacher.

7. *all ready, already*

   All ready (two separate words) means "everyone is ready."

   > The gym class is all ready to go on the field.

Already is an adverb meaning "even now" or "by or before this time."

> It was already time to leave.

8. *all right*

All right (always two separate words) means "everything is okay."

> Bill was all right after the accident.

Note: There is no such word as *alright*.

9. *all together, altogether*

All together means "everyone is together."

> We were all together in the auditorium.

Altogether is an adverb and means "completely."

> There was altogether too much noise in the classroom.

10. *among, between*

Among always implies three or more.

> I divided the candy among my four friends.

Between always means two.

> I divided the candy between Jack and me.

11. *anxious, eager*

Anxious implies "uneasiness, worry, or fear." Never use *anxious* for *eager*.

> She was anxious about her father's health.

Eager means "desire or interest."

> We were eager to go to the game.

12. *amount, number*

Amount suggests "bulk or weight."

> We collected a considerable amount of clothing for the poor.

Number is used for items that can be counted.

> The number of days before summer vacation is ten.

13. *apt, likely*

Apt means "quick to learn."

> Tom is an apt student.

Likely means "possible."

> It is likely to rain tomorrow.

14. *beside, besides*

Beside means "close to" or "at the side of."

> She sat beside me during the entire performance.

Besides means "in addition to."

> Besides my parents, my friends will also attend the ceremony.

15. *bring, take*

Bring means "to carry from a distant place to a nearer one."

> Please bring these books to my office.

Take means "to carry from a near place to a distant one."

> Please take these books to the library.

16. *continual, continuous*

    Continual implies repeated action.

    > I can't finish my work with these continual interruptions.

    Continuous implies that the action never stops.

    > He said he had a continuous buzzing in his head.

17. *datum, data*

    Datum is a seldom used Latin word meaning "factual material for research or discussion." It is singular and requires a singular verb.

    Data is plural, and either *data are* or *data is* may be used in popular writing; however, only *data are* is acceptable in scientific writing.

18. *different from*

    Use *different from,* not *different than.*

19. *disinterested, uninterested*

    Disinterested means "unbiased, not prejudiced, impartial."

    > A judge must be totally disinterested in the outcome of the case.

    Uninterested means "not interested, apathetic."

    > I am completely uninterested in the game.

20. *due to*

    Due to means "caused by." Use only when the words "caused by" can be logically substituted into the sentence.

    > His receiving two checks was due to an error. (caused by an error)

    > Due to a blowout, my car was wrecked. (better to use *because*)

21. *emigrate, immigrate*

    Emigrate means "to move out of or away from a country."

    > I emigrated from Russia in 1991.

    Immigrate means "to move into a country."

    > My parents immigrated to the United States ten years ago.

22. *enthusiastic, enthused*

    Enthusiastic means "eager about something, excited."

    > The team was enthusiastic about winning the Decathlon.

    Enthused is nonstandard and should not be used.

23. *in regard to*

    Always use *in regard to,* never *in regards to.*

24. *imply, infer*

    Imply refers to a meaning not stated but suggested in the original statement.

    > The weather report implied that a storm was near.

    Infer is used for a listener's or reader's judgment or conclusion based on the statement. A speaker implies; the listener infers.

    > My brother inferred from my actions that I was upset.

25. *irregardless*

    Irregardless is a nonstandard variant of *regardless.* Never use it in standard writing.

26. *farther, further*

    Farther always refers to distance.

    > We could go no farther on our journey that day.

    Further means "to a greater degree or extent" or "additional."

    > We had no further use for their help.

27. *fewer, less*

    Fewer is used when numbers can be counted.

    > Jane made fewer errors than I on the typing test.

    Less is used with quantities that cannot be counted.

    > This class needs less supervision.

28. *former, latter*

    Former refers to the first of two previously mentioned items.

    > The former of the two boys mentioned in the report is visiting his grandmother in Atlanta.

    Latter refers to the second of the two previously mentioned items.

    > The latter is going to England.

29. *healthful, healthy*

    Healthful gives health.

    > Arizona has a healthful climate.

    Healthy indicates that a person has health.

    > John is a healthy young boy.

30. *leave, let*

    Leave means "to allow to remain."

    > We will leave the book on the table.

    Let means "to permit."

    > Will you let me borrow your lawnmower?

31. *like, as*

    Like is a preposition.

    > She looks like her mother.

    As is a conjunction.

    > He is as tall as his father (is).

32. *rarely ever, seldom ever*

    In *rarely ever* and *seldom ever*, the *ever* is redundant. Do not say "He is rarely ever late," but "He is rarely late."

33. *try to*

    Try to should be used in place of *try and*.

    > He will try to discourage her from going to Europe this summer.

34. *unique*

    Unique means "one of a kind." It does not mean "odd" or "unusual." Because *unique* is "one of a kind", it is illogical to write *very unique, most unique,* or *extremely unique*.

35. *ways*

    Ways is plural. Never use it after the article *a*.

    > The hikers have a great way to go.

Correct Usage
Review 1

Part A.

Directions: The following sentences have problems in grammar, usage, diction (choice of words), and idioms. Some of the sentences are correct. No sentence contains more than one error. The error, if there is one, is underlined and lettered. Put the letter of the error on the line at the right. If there is no error, write *E*.

Example: <u>B</u>   She easily <u>adopted</u> to <u>her</u> <u>new</u> <u>environment</u>.
              A   B   C   D

_____ 1. <u>Everyone</u> of the students who <u>were</u> present <u>agree</u> that the best writer is <u>he</u>.
       A   B   C   D

_____ 2. She <u>angered</u> him <u>tremendously</u> when she <u>said</u> that he walks <u>like</u> his
       A   B   C   D
grandfather does.

_____ 3. If Tom <u>was</u> the president of the student body, I am <u>sure</u> that he would
             A   B
be <u>better</u> prepared than <u>she</u>.
   C   D

_____ 4. If Bob <u>would have</u> applied himself each day, he <u>would</u> not be in <u>danger</u>
               A   B   C
<u>of failing</u>.
  D

_____ 5. If the <u>loser</u> in the contest turns out to be <u>he</u>, <u>I shall have had</u> hardly <u>no</u>
       A   B   C   D
opportunity to speak with him.

_____ 6. <u>At that time</u> the United States <u>had seemed</u> to be <u>more powerful</u> than
      A   B   C
<u>any country</u> in the world.
  D

_____ 7. All members of the <u>administration</u> agreed that <u>each</u> member of the class
                    A   B
<u>may receive</u> credit for <u>his</u> participation in the contest.
  C   D

_____ 8. John is one <u>who</u> seems to like Helen better <u>than</u> <u>us</u>, <u>irregardless</u> of how
             A   B C   D
much we try to please him.

_____ 9. That <u>there</u> is <u>a</u> army of ants devouring my lunch <u>would have</u> come to
       A B   C
my attention sooner or <u>later</u>.
                 D

_____ 10. I do not want to <u>leave</u> the book <u>lie</u> on the floor without telling you and
                   A   B
<u>her</u> that you <u>had better</u> pick it up.
  C   D

_____11. <u>Providing</u> you listen carefully, you <u>will</u> be able to do the work as well as
          A   B
      <u>I</u> without any assistance from <u>them</u>.
      C   D

_____12. The clouds <u>obscured</u> <u>our</u> view of the earth below; <u>consequently</u>, we had
                   A   B   C
      <u>to solely rely</u> upon the instruments.
         D

_____13. We all <u>thought</u> that the <u>best</u> player on the basketball <u>team</u> to be <u>he</u>.
             A   B   C   D

_____14. My <u>brothers-in-law's</u> storage <u>facilities</u> far <u>exceeds</u> <u>ours</u>.
             A   B   C   D

_____15. <u>This</u> is one of the <u>tables</u> <u>that is</u> <u>to be fixed</u> next week.
     A   B   C   D

_____16. <u>Being</u> that neither John <u>nor</u> I <u>am</u> excused from practice, we will not
      A   B   C
      <u>be able</u> to go to the concert.
      D

_____17. Mrs. <u>Jones's</u> method of teaching <u>is</u> different <u>than</u> yours; I can learn
            A   B   C
      <u>better</u> in her class.
      D

_____18. Here <u>come</u> the group of players who <u>are</u> to hold an exhibition <u>match</u> in
         A   B   C
      our <u>gym</u>.
         D

_____19. It is <u>I</u> who <u>am</u> to <u>ever</u> stand between you and <u>him</u>.
         A   B   C   D

_____20. <u>We all</u> felt <u>badly</u> over the accident <u>that</u> occurred last week at the old <u>mill</u>.
      A   B   C   D

_____21. If you <u>lie</u> all your belongings on the <u>couch</u>, I will <u>be able</u> to determine
         A   B   C
      <u>whether</u> you need anything extra.
      D

       22. There <u>are</u> certainly <u>less</u> errors <u>being</u> made in our typing class since we
              A   B   C
      started <u>to use</u> the new keyboard.
           D

_____23. When you <u>spoke</u> yesterday at the meeting, <u>were</u> you <u>inferring</u> that Bob
              A   B   C
      is the <u>better</u> player of the two?
           D

_____24. If you <u>would have listened</u> to me, I <u>am</u> sure that the accident could have
        A   B   C
been <u>averted</u>.
            D

_____25. I <u>doubt</u> <u>if</u> I can go with you tomorrow; <u>my</u> mother is very <u>ill</u>.
       A   B   C   D

Part B.

Directions: Underline the errors in the following sentences and write the correct form. If there are no errors, write *correct*.

Example: *already*   They were <u>all</u> <u>ready</u> there.

_____26. If you would have moved the car on time, we would not have received a ticket.

_____27. This condenser was just installed, therefore, you should check the parts before installing them.

_____28. Irregardless of what she says, I cannot go at this time.

_____29. Of the two players, Paul is certainly the best.

_____30. She inferred from John's remarks that you are leaving town.

_____31. There are less items to be checked today.

_____32. She is one of the delegates who was chosen to attend.

_____33. No one, including Mary and I, have the right to make the decision for him.

_____34. The data that he collected was poor in quality.

_____35. The reason he lost is because he injured his shoulder.

_____36. Being that you won the writing contest, you are excused from writing your next paper.

_____37. She is a much better player than Tom or me.

_____38. Working to finish on time, I missed my lunch break.

_____39. I wish that I was able to help him at this time.

_____40. Sarah is as kind if not kinder than her sister.

Correct Usage
Review 2

Part A.

Directions: The following sentences have problems in grammar, usage, diction (choice of words), and idiom. Some of the sentences are correct. No sentence contains more than one error. The error, if there is one, is underlined and lettered. Put the letter of the error on the line at the right; if there is no error, write E.

Example: _D_   Either you <u>will tell</u> <u>her</u> <u>and</u> I will.
            A   B   C   D

_____ 1. It <u>is</u> very difficult to determine the exact time of the accident; moreover, the
            A
          <u>number</u> of people involved <u>make it</u> much more <u>difficult</u> for us to perform.
            B   C   D

_____ 2. <u>Everyone</u> wanted <u>us</u> to give <u>them</u> the report <u>immediately</u>.
            A   B   C   D

_____ 3. Neither you <u>nor</u> I <u>are</u> capable of <u>ridding</u> the city of this <u>unhealthful</u>
                      A   B   C   D
          situation.

_____ 4. Please <u>take</u> the result here <u>so that</u> the committee can examine the <u>details</u>
                  A   B   C
          for <u>themselves</u>.
              D

_____ 5. Ted with his two brothers <u>are</u> in the lobby <u>waiting</u> to talk <u>with</u> you
                                    A   B   C
          about a <u>possible</u> Christmas dance.
                  D

_____ 6. Not <u>aware of</u> the seriousness of the accident, <u>I was</u> <u>completely</u> <u>disinterested</u>
               A   B   C   D
          in their tale of woe.

_____ 7. In <u>typing</u> for a <u>winner's</u> trophy, you must endeavor to type <u>at</u> top speed
             A   B   C
          with <u>less</u> errors.
               D

_____ 8. The laboratory practices of <u>contemporary</u> scientists <u>relies</u> <u>heavily</u> <u>with</u>
                                      A   B   C   D
          those in charge of the operation.

_____ 9. Tom <u>is</u> <u>seldom ever</u> wrong when he decides <u>to choose</u> <u>an</u> assistant.
              A   B   C   D

_____ 10. This is <u>just</u> <u>one</u> of the many tires that <u>is</u> <u>being shipped</u> to Alaska.
                  A   B   C   D

_____ 11. We <u>all</u> <u>knew</u> of <u>you</u> leaving to take a <u>better</u> job in Africa.
             A   B   C   D

_____ 12. After the play, <u>each</u> member of the cast knew the <u>vandal</u> <u>was</u> <u>her</u>.
                       A   B C D

_____ 13. This <u>is</u> my final <u>remark</u>: the solution to the mystery <u>lays</u> right <u>before</u>
           A   B   C   D
your eyes.

_____ 14. If the coach <u>would have</u> listened to the <u>complaints</u> <u>earlier</u>, he
                            A   B   C
<u>would not have</u> this serious problem right now.
        D

_____ 15. There is <u>hardly</u> <u>no</u> reason for <u>his</u> acting in the way he <u>does</u>.
               A   B   C   D

_____ 16. Working all night <u>to finish</u> the quilt for the exhibition <u>my fingers</u> could
                               A   B
<u>hardly</u> <u>wrap</u> the finished product.
  C   D

_____ 17. Go <u>slow</u>, <u>don't</u> be hasty, and <u>you</u> won't have <u>no</u> regrets.
             A   B   C   D

_____ 18. <u>Everyone</u> in the room <u>was</u> extremely happy <u>which</u> <u>certainly</u> pleased the
           A   B   C   D
teacher.

_____ 19. The class <u>not only</u> was happy over the outcome, but also <u>satisfied</u> that a
                 A   B
<u>difficult</u> project <u>was finished</u>.
  C   D

_____ 20. Here <u>is</u> another one of those items <u>that</u> <u>has been</u> the <u>basis</u> for his
           A   B C   D
failure as a salesman.

_____ 21. This <u>problem</u> should <u>not only</u> be considered <u>by</u> the senior class, <u>but</u> also
             A   B   C   D
by the junior class as well.

_____ 22. He <u>was advised</u> to <u>obtain</u> an application blank, <u>and</u> that
           A   B   C
<u>he should complete it</u> as soon as possible.
       D

_____ 23. I want <u>to advise</u> you that <u>your</u> insisting that the set of papers
                A   B
<u>were corrected</u> without supervision <u>is</u> unwise.
  C   D

_____ 24. My brother has been <u>laying</u> down on the <u>couch</u> all morning; we decided
                         A   B   C
<u>to take</u> him to the hospital.
  D

_____ 25. Our mayor <u>has</u> <u>always</u> had a deep interest <u>for</u> <u>youth's</u> struggle for identity.
                 A B   C D

Part B.

Directions: Underline the errors in the following sentences and write the correct form. If there are no errors, write *Correct.*

Example: <u>affected</u>   Jeff's answers <u>effected</u> his grade.

_____ 26. The team was very enthused over its victory against Fillmore.

_____ 27. Please bring these books there as soon as possible.

_____ 28. The climate in California is very healthy.

_____ 29. Her mumbling aggravated the teacher.

_____ 30. There was all together too much disturbance at the rally.

_____ 31. Do you think it will be alright to send the report later?

_____ 32. We were all anxious to attend the football game on Saturday.

_____ 33. It is almost impossible for the President to affect changes in the White House.

_____ 34. It is all ready time to close the gym.

_____ 35. Between Mary, Tom, and me, there can never be a strong friendship.

_____ 36. If you don't wish to irritate your cold, take plenty of rest.

_____ 37. I was completely disinterested in the movie we saw last week.

_____ 38. There was alot of packages on the table.

_____ 39. The building is apt to be unsafe during an earthquake.

_____ 40. All the data collected last week is no longer relevant.

The Publisher

All instructional materials identified by the TAP® (Teachers/Authors/Publishers) trademark are developed by a national network of 460 teacher-authors, whose collective educational experience distinguishes the publishing objective of The Center for Learning, a nonprofit educational corporation founded in 1970.

Concentrating on values-related disciplines, the Center publishes humanities and religion curriculum units for use in public and private schools and other educational settings. Approximately 600 language arts, social studies, novel/drama, life issues, and faith publications are available.

Publications are regularly evaluated and updated to meet the changing and diverse needs of teachers and students. Teachers may offer suggestions for development of new publications or revisions of existing titles by contacting

The Center for Learning
Administration/Editorial
29313 Clemens Road, Suite 2E
Westlake, OH 44145
(440) 250-9341 • FAX (440) 250-9715

For a free catalog containing order and price information and a descriptive listing of titles, contact

The Center for Learning
Customer Service
590 E. Western Reserve Rd., Unit 10-H
Youngstown, OH 44514
(800) 767-9090 • FAX (888) 767-8080
http://www.centerforlearning.org